Un...ck Your
Money Blocks!

101 SELF-LIMITING BELIEFS AROUND MONEY

The intent of this book is to help you look at and review your money beliefs systems. If you have ever struggled with money, this material will help you. Our beliefs create our reality, and when we change our beliefs about money, our experiences change. It's about changing the perceptions of the experiences we are having. When the perception changes, then the reality changes.

Many of us have been programmed with negative money belief systems. We get them through media, parents, school, our peers, and from the bombardment of information that bounces around in the world. When we clear the negative belief systems, it makes room to anchor new positive money belief systems.

It is said, "persistence pays off." The more you practice, the easier it gets. It's about getting into the flow and keeping the flow going. It's about what you focus on. I've personally used these techniques in my life, and for me, I've received miracles... Give it a try. The success you can have is unlimited! There is no telling what you can do... It's up to you! This is 101 ways to unlock your money blocks and to help you find your true money potential. Find the beliefs that are blocking you, and then work to transform these beliefs. These techniques can be used in other areas of your life too. Get the Law of Attraction to work for you! Have Fun!

1

Money is the root of all evil.

It was not said that money is the root of all evil, but , "The love of money is the root of evil."

Money itself is not good or bad.
Money doesn't think when you look at it.
It's how we think about money that affects our money experiences.

Forgive it.

Exercise

Forgive yourself for where you are at in your situation. This book is about shifting focus and thinking.

Give yourself credit for being here. Write down your own negative money beliefs, be prepared to get rid of them.

2

Money doesn't grow on trees.

It was always said, not sure by who...
the adage money doesn't grown on trees... meaning it's hard to come by...

You have to work long hard grueling hours.
There's a shortage of supply is implied...the feeling of lack. Some success experts talk about growing your money tree....

Others talk about infinite supply. When it comes down to it, it's a feeling.

Build an Alter.

Exercise

Make a money shrine.

Even if it starts with a couple of pennies.
I've even had pictures of real money around.
Some people talk about carrying a hundred that you don't spend.

In Feng Shui, money is placed in a certain part of the home to keep it flowing.
I leave change piles around in spots, sometimes with a couple of bucks on them. The idea is to start seeing it.
Start feeling like you have it.
Start getting comfortable with money.
Use your intuition.

Make it fun. You are not praying to
it. You are affirming having it.

3

Money is hard to get.

This rolls off of #2, but it is all
connected.
Lack thinking, shortage.
Not seeing it, the money and
abundance you already have.

Again, it feels like the coding we got
during times of depression.
Not enough, as soon as you have it,
it disappears.
It's a matter of shifting thinking,
there are plenty of ways to make
money.

If you want it you'll get it.
Start expecting money.
Many money masters talk about becoming a money magnet.

Watch Your Words.

Exercise

Start noticing how you speak about money.

Listen to how the people around you talk about it.
What attitudes about money were going on in the first 7 years of your life? Even the feeling your parents had can affect your money attitudes.
Some of this might be uncomfortable.
It's going get better.
We're clearing negative money beliefs.
Ask yourself to look at it from a detached emotional perspective.

This means reviewing it, but not re-experiencing it or feeling it. Remember your best money times. Find what they call an anchor point, a birthday, a graduation, your best moments. Anytime you get down, you can remember the good moments and feelings to pull you out of it.

4

There's not enough money to go around.

This is another phrase we've all heard. It has been coded into many of us.

This is about uncovering the unconscious self-limiting beliefs in

the unconscious. Shortage... Not
enough, a belief to get rid of.

Enough is Enough.

Exercise

"I am enough."

Repeat this to yourself.
Say it to yourself in your eyes in the
mirror.
Tap your heart say it out loud.
Do this as often as you can.
Anytime you start to go into lack,
remind yourself.
"I am enough."
You can add, "I have enough."
Just keep anchoring this into you.
Ask your higher-self
to start working in your
subconscious mind to change your
programming.

5

You can never have enough money.

This is sort of confusing.
Do we want a lot? How much is enough?

How much is too much?
Are you setting parameters and limits?
What do you want, can handle, and are willing to do to get our desired outcome?
A question to investigate in your own planning about money, and our expectation of it.

Expect Miracles.

Exercise

Start expecting money.

Ask your higher-self to go in your future, and bring you money miracles…
Unexpected checks, rebates, change on the ground.
We get into this later, but you having money doesn't take away from other people having money.
Your gain is not someone else's loss... atleast not in the way honest way we're talking about manifesting it.
Imagine having money right now. The longer you can hold that focus, then you attune with it. From there, the steps to getting it are easier.
Get into the space of gratitude.
Start seeing that you already have money. Expect it.

6

Rich people are corrupt.

There is a spiritual connection with this historically.
It's the rich get richer attitude, and thew belief system that money is bad.

This system that tries to keep the little guy down. It can be shifted out of if you don't let it into you.

You are enough.
You always have what you need.
You are the one creating your supply.

Not all money people are corrupt.
This is the negative stereotype.
If you have these sort of beliefs

systems. They could be blocking your flow of money..." I don't want money...it will corrupt me."
This is wrong thinking that will unconsciously stop you fro making money.
If you believe money is good, a blessing, you deserve it, and you're worth it... Money is just a blessing then...there is no corruption.

Change the Movie.

Exercise

Think about where you got this belief from.
Media, conditioning, and news, we tend to hear more of the negative than the positive. Looking on the bright side takes practice.
Meditate on what happened to you as a child concerning money. Whatever pops on the screen in your mind...change the movie.

Imagine getting apologized to for whatever happened.
Then change the movie...
Make it how you wish it would have been and how you want it to be now.
Come to a place of forgiveness of the past.
Hold the feeling of how you wanted it to be.
At this point, your unconscious doesn't know the difference.
I explain to people, "Many have told a white lie until it became a true story to themself."
Do this with your past...
After years of studying, and in my own life, this is one of the most powerful techniques I think there is.
Change the movie memory in your mind to something positive.

7

Having money is greedy.

This type of thinking goes into the belief that you having money is somehow taking away from me having money… That there is this competition, and if you have others won't.

On the other level, it is up to the individual.

It's not greedy to have all you ever dreamed of.

You do have to work for it, but if you do what you love the money will come. This is what all great success experts talk about. You can do it...believe in yourself first.

Piece of Cake.

Exercise

Make peace with it.

There are greedy people, but there are also plenty enlightened millionaires. You can have.
Others can have.
The idea is win win for everybody.
Open your heart to receiving.
Start allowing yourself to have money.
Tap your heart and say, "I am worthy of having money."
"Money will allow me to be a more generous person."

8

It's not spiritual having money.

The belief that the material is bad. There's a lot of spiritual people caught up on this. I was caught up on this.

It goes back to one... that money is somehow this negative dark thing. That money is bad to have, and that it turns you bad.

Plenty of good people have money, and many of them do a lot to help other people. The new dimension is about lifting each other up...

Get a positive attitude about money...

Make peace with it.

Money is only the energy that you give it.

Change the Thermostat.

Exercise

Make money spiritual.

Serge Kahili King, Huna Philosopher talks about being the Emperor of the Universe. Imagine that you own everything.
Every car on the road is yours.
You own the buildings.
In divine essence...
You are everything.
This imagination puts you in the feeling of having.
Notice how you act.
Notice how others respond to you.
Refine how you are going to be with lots of money.
Experts talk about, "Raising the glass ceiling."
This means where your

subconscious set at.
A Visualization of a thermostat just came to me.
Turn it up.
If you make a hundred a day...
Imagine making $1000/day
Set your own thermostat for where your money is at.

9

Only some people get to have money.

This is the belief that some people are selected for it.
Like you have to be born into it, and have to be born lucky...like it's a gene. It's actually because of unconscious conditioning.
It's true environment and who you hang out with have to do with it.

If you hang out at the tattoo shop...
you eventually get a tattoo.
If you hang out with people with
money, you begin to adopt their
attitudes and beliefs. It tends to be a
positive energy.

Tap it in.

Exercise

Tap your heart and remind yourself
you are a money person. It's ok to
be a money person.
Money is not bad.
It goes along with self-worth and
self-esteem.
Tap your heart and say out loud.
"I am a money person... money
comes to me."
"I am safe, and I am free"...
"I always have plenty of money."
Start creating your own money
affirmations.
This is a process of clearing the

negative, and anchoring the positive.
Take your time, but don't be
complacent.
With all reprogramming, persistence
is the key.
Start thinking that money is on it's
way to you.
You have enough, and more is
showing up.

10

You have to work hard to make a lot of money.

It's true...on some level you do.
Some people have programmed
themselves to win the lottery. I'm not
guarantying that, but even that took
the person work.
One guy on youtube one the lottery

twice.

Others say, "We all deserve to win the lottery at least once."

It doesn't mean you have to work countless hours at a dead end job...that's why they call em dead end jobs.

Some jobs are great to get you through, but you have to think bigger. Carve your niche and be creative... a lot of people do a couple of different things. Figure out ways to get passive income generated.

Be specific.

Exercise

Write down exactly how much you want to have. Make it detailed, the more detailed the better.

This goes for anything you want to manifest, not only money. Put it present tense, like you already have

it.
Make it real and ad the feeling.
For example:
"Thank God I continuously earn $1000/day."
"It's fun and easy and feels great."
"I'm doing what love, and it's easier than I thought it would be." Make your own, set your own parameters.

Go beyond, and let the sky be the limit.
The reason the present tense is important is because it gets into, "Now." You have it now!

11

My prosperity takes away from others.

I sort of touched on this,
but it's the concept that me having
money takes away from you having
money and vice versa… Then I
might be greedy, or someone else
might need it more than me. There's
plenty of people that will take it if
you're rejecting it on some level.

Anything is possible.

Exercise

Get into the concept that money is
unlimited. It comes from nothing in
the imagination.
They say there is no difference
between one dollar and 1 million

dollars. It's just the mind that thinks there is a difference.

The mind thinks a million is a lot more that a buck.

They both come from nothing.

This is why raising the thermostat and the glass ceiling is important.

Welcome and accept that there is plenty for all.

If you can have anything you want to ask for more.

If you get into the Abraham-Hicks material, they talk about hoping focus. We try to manifest it, but as soon as we don't get it… We fall back into lack. The trick is to keep seeing it. Just hold focus. If you didn't get it on the first day, it does't mean you won't get it. Just keep thinking you already have it. Make a plan and take action steps.

12

If I spend money, I won't have any money.

This implies that you'll run out if you buy the things you want.
This doesn't mean go and over spend, but as soon as you start thinking lack, it can block your flow. Others believe you can bless the money you spend, and ten times that amount comes back. In tithing, people donate a percentage of what they are earning as a from of gratitude. It is an act designed to be grateful for enough and more coming.
It's also an act of keeping the flow going.

Bless it!

Exercise

Start blessing the money you have.

As you spend it, expect ten times that amount in return. Ask your unconscious mind to do this for you. Visualize it showing up.
Keep imagining the flow.
As you send it out more comes back to you. Imagine a money ocean and waves of money coming to you.

13

You have to struggle to survive.

This has been in us since we were cave men, because that's what we had to do... constantly adapt, since hunting and gathering.

Go out and get it.

In the Law of Attraction, you still have to take action steps. It's not about being in panic about it.

It's about faking it till you make it.

Feel it till you have it.

Keep feeling the feeling of having money.

Don't go into fear and thinking that you're running low. When this happens, catch yourself.

Start back on thinking you have enough.

Give yourself a silver spoon.

Exercise

This can be any spoon, but one to remind you to remind yourself.

I've told people with low self-esteem to hang up gold stars to remind themselves they are doing a good job.

The silver spoon idea just came to me.

You don't have to struggle.

You might not have been born with one, but that doesn't mean you can't have one. Imagine it. What would it be like to have all of the things you want? What would it be like to have it be easy?

You still have to work.

It's the perception that work sucks. Imagine having enough that you don't have to work.

The ones that created millions love what they do...
That's why they can do it all of the time.
The silver spoon is a reminder that you can have the life of your dreams too. You still have to do something.
This is designed to start awakening and activating your subconscious.
You can and will have it.
You already have it.
The silver spoon reminds you that you are your own golden goose.

14

Money causes problems.

I guess it does if you believe that.
If you think it's greedy, will make you evil, cause you hassles and fights

with people... lawsuits...having it and losing it.

These are all fears that can unconsciously prevent you from allowing money to show up.

Inside Job

Exercise

Bless your future,
Ask your guides and angels to bless your future.
Ask that it never be a problem for you.
View money as a blessing.
This is not to say that we are putting everything on having a lot of money.
Give yourself permission to have enough.
Feel good about yourself whether you have it not.
When you feel good about yourself,
You won't be afraid to begin attracting it to you.

Look at your relationships.
It's ultimately about your relationship with yourself.
Tap your heart and say, "I love myself."
Know you are a lovable person.
Create a belief that money loves you and that it makes all of your relationships better. It's not a dependency on something outside of you.
It's a feeling within that you externalize.

15

If I have money I'll lose it.

This is just to reiterate belief systems to look at.
If it causes problems... It's all beliefs

based in fear, so they are all
unconnected on some level.
The good news is that once you
recognize them, you can let them
go.

Liquid Money

Exercise

Think of a time when you had
money and lost it. Think of all the
stories you hear about successful
people that lose it. Decide that you
won't be one of those people.
Start educating yourself on how to
save and keep it,
how to get the flow going and go
from a trickle to a waterfall. Imagine
a waterfall of money...
The Universe is pouring blessings
upon you.
Affirm:

"I am good with money."
"I am able to keep and save money."
"I'm always in the proper money flow."

16

God must not want me to have money.

If you've been around a lot of lack and limitation, or grew up in poverty, it is possible to adopt the attitude that God doesn't want you to have money. That you're not supposed to have it.

That you're somehow being punished.

It still goes to some sort of belief that money is bad, or that God thinks you're bad.

This is the furthest from the truth.

Imagine God as an unconditionally loving being...

God's Grace

Exercise

Imagine God picking you up and hugging you. Apologizing for all you have been through.
View God as an unconditional loving being.
God still loves you.
You just had to learn some lessons.
Ask to have your lessons learned through grace and ease. Know you are not forgotten.
God hasn't forgotten you.
Meditate and ask why am I creating lack for myself?
"What is the belief that is causing it."
Write the negative belief in your note book under the negative beliefs.
Write a new positive belief for yourself.

17

If I have money people will be jealous.

It's true. In the realm of money, there is a lot of competition. Especially if you believe that it's a cut throat game, and that you have to be a shark to get it. If there is an over flowing cup... there is enough for all. Some talk about not viewing money as way of keeping score.
If you fear people coveting what you have,
that people will be jealous... family members, friends, the people you know. Then you could be limiting your flow of money.

"Water off a Duck's Back."

Exercise

On some level, it's probably because we are jealous of people with money. As spiritual people, everything with-out is a reflection of within.
Are you jealous of people with money.
Have you had past people jealous of you about money.
Don't let that bother you.
It's about being thick skinned.
Many of us are sensitive.
That doesn't mean you have to enter the shark tank...
Wall Street may not be your place, but that doesn't mean you can't have money. See people congratulating you for having money again.
See yourself as not being bothered by what other people think of you.

People may be jealous, don't let that stop you.

18

If I have money people will just want me for my money.

This is the gold digger fear...the fear that people will be fake and phony… That they'll just like you because you have money. It stems from a self-esteem issues and self-confidence belief systems. You have to buy your friends. The fear that, " Money can't buy love."
That even if you have money, you won't be able to trust any real people.

Anchoring Self Love.

Exercise

When you begin to love yourself you resonate with others who love themselves. Trust that you will know who his real and who isn't.
We all intuitively do this all of the time.
Forgive yourself for creating this belief system.
See yourself as being able to protect your wealth.
Get out of the need to act like you have a lot and foot the bill.
Ask your angels to help you remove this fear.
When you shift within, and view yourself as having...
You'll attract others that view themselves as having.
There won't be an issue if you don't believe there will be one.

19
Money Can't buy love.

As I write this, it all flows together.
I made the list, and now I'm backing
it up. These are some of my
personal beliefs I had to uncover.
When I look at what's next on the
list, it correlates to what the last one
is about. I am noticing a flow within
the limiting side of money.
The idea is to get into the flow with
the positive side of money.

Love Yourself First

Exercise

You don't need to buy love if you
have self love. If you have to buy

love, it's phony.
You're lovable with or without money.
Keep imagining being lovable.
You begin to attract new friends.
First, imagine yourself as having lots of love.
Think of a team of angels coming to permeate you with love.
It comes from above and percolates within you.
Imagine that you're a fountain of love vibrations flowing through you.
No one will want to buy it from you, because it can't be sold. This is helping anchor the good feeling.
It's the feeling of love.
This is what we replace having lots of money with.
"If I have lots of money, then I'll be lovable."
It's a feeling not the money.
Love is free.
It's true, "Money can't buy it."

You can have love without money.
I don't think the love of money is bad either.
It's when we turn it into greed and corruption…
When it rules our lives.
These are just other fears.
Decide you will be fearless around money.

20

I'm not good with money.

If you say that, the Universe won't give it to you. There is also a part that doesn't want it. The part that believes it's too much work, or you'll squander it... It just disappears.
If you've had past struggles or negative experiences with money,

the fear of it happening again could be holding you back from money action.

You're Great With Money!

Exercise

Decide you will become a great money manager. Learn about money.
Forgive your past.
When you're good with it, then the Universe will give it to you. You have to show the Universe first.
Start making it fun and easy.
Affirm: Tap your heart and say…
"I am great with money."
"I am able to handle large quantities of money."
"I am the money I am seeking."

21

I can't save money.

This applies to the spendaholics and impulse buyers. This can be shifted if you recognize it.

It's not about going out for sushi every night.
The wealthy are always figuring out ways to save money, conserve, and cut corners. Some people save all of their change...

Fill a milk jug...it ads up.
It's about feeling like you have some.
It's a sense of security.
Money itself is tangible, but itself doesn't think.
We could get out there on some yogi

everything is a living being types stuff, I'm into it. However, we're not here to pontificate the thoughts of a Ferrari...

You think… it's how you think about money.

The wealthy don't go out for coffee or lunch everyday...

Some do, but while you're in the process of getting there, there is some sacrifice involved.

"Attractor Factor"

Exercise

Skip going out for the coffee, and throw the money in a jar.

Make a pot at home for a fraction of the price.

Stay home from the bar.

Get a movie at the library.

Figure out all of the ways you can start saving money.

Go back to the time when you had

the most savings… Know you've accomplished that, so you can do it again.

It's within you. Save the change in the jar where you can see it. Take ten percent of what you bring in and save it.

Make it your money magnet.

This attracts more to it.

Release the need to spend all of your money.

Catch yourself on impulse buying.

Practice saving until it is second nature.

22

I never have enough money.

I know the feeling. I've been there. It can make you angry, stressed,

depressed, and cause anxiety.
On the yogi level, this means you are not resonating the truth that you always have enough.
It's again, on a core level, recognizing that you're in fear.
On a cosmic level, there are only two things fear or love... all the negative money beliefs are fear based.
If you recognize it as fear then you can correct it.
We can talk about that later. There are several techniques designed to help you get out of fear, and step back into love. It's not the love of money, it's the absence of fear.
Successful people do everything eventhough they are afraid. A great master taught, "Fear is my friend."
If you're afraid if something; go do it, then you won't be afraid of it.

I used to be afraid of the dark...then I slept in a pitch black room till it

didn't scare me. I've tied a blindfold on and stumbled around the house on my own. Taoist say this helps dissolve the ego.
Face your fear dissolve it!

Always Have More Than Enough Money.

Exercise

You already have enough now.
Make a gratitude list of all you have that you are grateful for.
Shift focus.
When I believe I never have enough, I get unexpected bills.
When I think I have enough, I get unexpected checks.
Imagine your account having exactly how much you want in it.
Then, meditate on what you have to do to get it.
Make a list and start taking action

steps.

The entire time, hold focus that you already have the amount that you want. While you're in the process, the fear and panic will try fro creep in.

If you believe you'll get it, you'll get it.

If you know you'll get it, you'll get it a lot quicker.

23

It's more spiritual being poor.

This has historical, and if you believe in them, past life connotations. Mother Theresa loved serving the poor.

It feels noble to help.

The truth is… You being poor isn't

helping the poor.
If you have money you can help people.

It's not good or bad.

Exercise

Imagine what you are going to do to help people. You can only have so many houses and trips around the world. What are you going to do to make a difference and help lift people up. Then, you can give back. See it as shifted.
As if you did it.
Create a new belief that it is spiritual having money.
You will do it, just keep believing it.

24

Money makes the world go round.

The world is spinning. Money is not the reason. I'm looking at my own belief and asking why it limited me. It stems off of money as this thing to covet. Some have it some don't. That it's bad to be in the money game. That it takes away from your spirituality. Others believe making money is spiritual.

The more people you help the more money you make... even that is a belief system. The bottom line is we are free to create our own belief systems. When we are not achieving our own goals, the first question to ask is, why? When you find the belief the prevents you, eliminate it.

Then, you can begin to create what you want.

On the root core level, remember to focus on what you want rather than what you don't want. Again, we get what we focus on.

Conscious Creation

Exercise

Create your own luck. Imagine being lucky. Reprogram yourself for things to work out. Remind yourself to expect miracles. If you don't believe in miracles, Ask for a miracle to help you believe. Believe you are a miracle. Life is a miracle. Believe you are lucky.

25

Rich people are stuck-up.

This is an elitism belief system where rich people are all better than everyone else. Money is this thing that makes people all egotistical. It's true it can do that to some people. If you fear it happening to you, you could be preventing yourself from having it. It still goes back to simplest terms... Focusing that you don't have it, and if you do, it will make you a bad person.
The belief that money is a competition. The fear that money is a click that won't let you in. It hinges off of the separation thing.

Create your own click.

Exercise

See yourself as being welcomed.
Give yourself permission to have
money.
Start your own money manifestation
group. Hang out with some people
who have money, and find out they
are not all bad people. Most of them
are down to earth. Stop beating
yourself up for not having money, It's
only temporary.
Money welcomes you.
Welcome money into your
awareness.
Just keep holding the feeling that
you are alright. Meditate on what
you can do to turn things around.
Imagine it being all turned around for
the better.

26

Rich people think they are better than everyone.

It's because it's all based off of self-worth.
It's not that they think they are better, it's because they have strong self-esteem. They value themselves.
They worked to get what they have.
It is time and energy... figuring out how to optimize everything.
It's that we don't feel good enough about ourselves.
Or it's that we have good feelings about ourselves,
and have had an abusive boss or money figure in our lives.
I've taken it back to the conditioning

of shows like the Flintstones, Honeymooners, and other television. It on a certain level is an old paradigm.

The conditioning that the job sucks, the boss is abusive, and we have to just muddle through. Ask to have that cleared from your subconscious.

If you are going through this, this is designed to help you clear that programing.

Shield it.

Exercise

Say a prayer.
Put yourself in a green bubble of light.
Ask that you can express yourself, and that it doesn't hurt anyone involved. This is just a releasing process.
Write down all of the negative

money feelings that come up now.
It's about getting to a deeper level.
Forgive society for how it has gotten.
Stop blaming the system.
Release the resentment toward
wealth and money.
See yourself come to a place of
forgiveness and peace. The process
of writing it down is more powerful
than just thinking about it. Once you
have your list of negative beliefs.
Say a prayer and thank it.
Then get rid of it.
Say another prayer to your angels
and unconscious mind to help you
release it. Do a ritual of your own.
I have a burning bowl and burn
them. Sometimes I tear them up
and flush them. It's the act of letting
it go on the unconscious level. Then
write down what your life is like now
that you are making money. Write
down how you are making it and
how much you are making. Use a

level that stretches your imagination, but you believe is possible.
The unconscious mind likes specifics.
Don't just ask for more money.
If you're making $100/day
Ask for $1000/day
Jumping to a million a day might be too much of a stretch at first. It's still totally possible.

27

I have to feel guilty for having money.

This goes back to believing that money for you takes away from money from others. Therefore, guilt for having. Believing quick money and massive amounts are bad. The true experts take their time and build it up.

They get to the point where they make their money work for them. If you believe money is bad, you'll feel guilty for having. Then you'll block yourself.

Hopefully, we've done some clearing around this.

Click the switch.

Exercise

Imagine a switch in your mind…
The fuse box or control room.
Click the switch that says, "Guilt around money." off. There is no reason to have guilt around money.
Having it allows you more comfort.
Click on the switch that says, "Comfortable around money."
It's that easy. Do it as often as needed.

28

It's a hassle having money.

All the bills, all of the paper work.
Money can seem boring... the
logistics.
For creative and spiritual people,
the business part of it takes away
from meditating or creating. "I don't
want to do what it takes."
I've tried meditating on the rocks
that I'm a millionaire... In reality,
millionaires surround you and let you
know you aren't gonna get it that
way.
I'm a person who believes in Avatars
that can pour gold coins out of their
hands. Success experts talk about
having a plan and taking action
steps.

Grace and Ease.

Exercise

Make it easy. Make it fun.
Instead of paying your bills and
hating it.
Pay your bills with the gratitude that
you have the money to pay your
bills.   If you're in debt, imagine
being out of debt.
Be in a state of gratitude that it's all
worked out.
When you balance your checkbook,
Imagine having ten times that
amount.
Imagine what you're going to do with
the extra money.   Write yourself a
check for the amount you want to
have. Keep it where you can see it,
and focus on the feeling of it coming
too manifest. Do this as long as it
takes.

29

Money causes fights about money.

I know it sounds redundant or does it? If this aggravates you, it shows limiting beliefs about money. Napoleon Hill talks about positive anger.

Too many the book, "Think and Grow Rich" is a Bible. Right now, there are millions of millionaires in the process of bringing a new money paradigm...

Money doesn't have to be a fight or a struggle...

It can be an everybody thrive situation.

You deserve to have...the more you feel you deserve...

The more you have.

It's about how you think about yourself and what you are doing.

"Shake hands with the past."

Exercise

Forgive the past money battles. Whatever comes up on your radar screen,
see it as over. See them apologizing to you, apologize to them.
Thank them for the lesson. Whoever contributed to negative money beliefs.
See it the way, you wished it would have been and you want it to be now. Ask your higher-self to clear this program for you.
See money as a win win for everyone.

30

Rich people get there by taking advantage of others.

If it is, "Dog eat dog," and "Every man for himself," Then you may not want to be part of that game, because it amounts to anguish and hurt.
If everybody is screwing each other, and you've been screwed before...
Then you don't want to get in, because of the fear of the pain you went through. This gets into the concept of shifting the past. That's what we did in the last exercise. In psychology they call it reframing.
You change your memory of it.
I learned it from a Huna Shaman, and Phd Psychologists figured it out too. There is an importance to re-visualizing the past 50 times.

It's to re-anchor a new memory in the subconscious to get a new result.
Your subconscious doesn't know the difference. It just knows what you program into it.

Reframe.

Exercise

Reframe 50 times in your mind. Go through any negative past memories that are still lingering. Change the movie in your mind 50 times.
See it over and over.
Serge Kahili King taught me, 'if you stubbed your toe on a rock… see it 50 times where you didn't stub your toe." Change your memory. The key is to actually do it... (50 times.)

31

I'm not worthy of having money.

Wayne's World..."We're not worthy." We joke and put ourselves down to appear humble. The problem is the unconscious eventually believes it, so stop putting yourself down. Self-worth is what all success experts teach. First you have to believe you deserve it. Then be confident that you'll get it.

Worthy and Deserving.

Exercise

Click off the unworthy switch. Tap into your heart, "I am worthy and

deserving." See Wayne's World where they are exclaiming,
"We are worthy!"
"You are worthy!"
Meditate on what you can do to increase your self-worth. Do something nice for yourself. You deserve it!

32

There's not enough money in the Universe.

Basically, there's not enough thinking. The universe is unlimited. That's what we have to tap into. It's always available.

There is all this stuff out there about unlimited abundance. Start focusing on enough. Gratitude is a big key. It's about the feeling you are resonating.

When you start to go into fear... catch yourself and start focusing on gratitude. Start counting things to be grateful for. It keeps you focused on feeling good.

Infinite Universe

Exercise

Imagine everything… How much there is. Everywhere. It keeps expanding. Imagine the higher realms…

The place where money is unlimited. The place where everyone has enough. Find that feeling.

Ask for guidance there. What do you need to learn?

What do you need to change? Is there anything you need to know. Ask your own questions. Anchor the feeling of unlimited.
Ask it to filter down to you. Don't be afraid to ask for things you want.

33

I am separate from money.

You have to hunt and gather it thinking. Others believe it is inside you to be externalized. Believe in yourself. Think in terms of miracles... anything is possible. It's not outside you.
It comes down through you...ideas and action steps. Imagine that money flows through you... That it is inside you to be externalized.

If you are separate from it, then you are focused on lack.

In quantum physics, it's the observer theory... you get what you focus on.

In Ho' oponopono, energy flows where attention goes. Again, you get what you focus on.

Sun and Moon.

Exercise

Imagine that you are the money that you are seeking. Go inward and meditate.

It comes from within you to be externalized.

There is a meditation called the sun and moon meditation. I learned it from Dr. Pillai, and it comes from Siva Baba. It's on Youtube. You can look it up.

The easiest way to explain it is, You go into your heart chakra.

You imagine the Sun and the Moon. Merge them and imagine the timelessness of God. You are the Sun, and you are the Moon. You are the thing you are trying to manifest. You transcend time, by imagining that you are it. In essence, you have it right now. The longer you can hold this focus, The quicker you will manifest it. A Key is also, to let it go. Leave it up to the universe. Surrender to the guides and angels. Allow the ideas and action steps to fall into place. Abraham and the Abraham-Hicks material talks about this… As soon as you break focus you lost it… As soon as you go, "But I don't have it." ımagine the sun and moon in your heart. Hold focus on the thing you are trying to manifest. Project it out into your third eye a foot in front of your forehead. Find the feeling of it.
Sananda speaks of identifying with

it. Believe you already have it,
because you are it.

34

It's bad to want money.

The concept that spirituality and
money don't mix. Some spiritual
guru's teach you deserve to drive a
Mercedes. If you believe it's bad,
you'll block it.
If this pushes triggers, it's o.k.,
because we're going to clear them.
There's a part of you that wants
money, that's why this interests you.
Give yourself permission to enjoy
money and the comfort it brings.

Give yourself permission.

Exercise

Tap your heart.
Say, "I now accept money into my life."
"I give myself permission to have money." "Money is a tool used for good things." "It allows me to have more comfort in my life."

35

It's bad to have money.

Money is not bad, and people are people.
We tend to hear through news and media the negative side of money…

The corruption, greed, war, killing...money is the enemy. The system is trying to suppress us... Step out of it. Money welcomes you...
Create your own new beliefs around money.

Change the Channel.

Exercise

Think of the good people doing good things with money. Think of your happiest times with money.
Where did you create the belief it was bad.
What messages did you get.
Start changing the channel.
A technique you can use is imagine changing the channel on the radio station… The channel playing all of the negative money is bad tracks...
Change it to the channel playing money and abundance are good

tracks. Tell your unconscious to start listening and hearing new positive messages.

36

It's filthy being rich.

A common phrase we've all heard. Unconsciously anything you hear enough times we accept as a belief and truth. The truth is the unconscious doesn't know the difference, just what you tell it. It doesn't know past ,present, and future. This is how hypnosis works. Find positive money role models to inspire you. If you believe it's filthy being rich, you'll block it.

Take a money bath.

Exercise

You deserve it.
Wash clean off the filthy rich belief system.
Imagine the tub being filled with liquid gold.
It absorbs into your system, and feel your body soaking in wealth and luxury. Salt baths are a great way to cleanse your aura and negative emotions. Think of the water taking all of the lack and negativity out of you. When you drain the tub, imagine the negativity going out with it.
"You are no longer throwing your money down the drain."
Wash clean of the past, and become the person you want to be when it comes to money. You could also do this in the shower. Imagine the

water as drops of gold cleansing you. Imagine being showered in coins.
Have a fresh new money attitude!

37

Having Money Makes You Evil.

This goes back to number one.
The belief that money is this terrible thing...if it is evil... It will turn me evil by having it. Money is not taboo, it puts food on the table. It's not to be discouraged and feared. It's about re-igniting the spark.
Money will help you become a better person if you let it.

Make peace with money.

Exercise

Imagine money as a Grim Reaper.
Put the Grim Reaper on stage.
See the crowd booing and hissing.
See the Grim Reaper taking a bow.
Now, see an actor taking the costume off.
See it as a new money angel, nothing to be afraid of.
See the actor apologize to you for scaring you.
It was just a character in a play.
Thank that character for the lessons it taught you. Decide you will no longer be afraid when it comes to money. Develop your new money character.

38

I can't have money.

If you've had money and lost it, squandered it, haven't been good with it in the past... We tend to believe we just can't have it, that maybe we're not supposed to have it. It turns around quick when you shift focus.

Believe you can have money, God wants you to have money… there's enough money. Have gxratitude for the money you have now.
Make peace with it.

"Love is all you need."

Exercise

This is about self love and forgiveness. You can have money. Forgive yourself for your past money mistakes. Tap your heart and say,
"I forgive and love myself."
"I release my past with money."
"I can have money."
"I am able to handle having money."

39

Other people get to have money, but not me.

We see other people with all of this stuff. No one taught us how to get it. It becomes a separation thing again.

The ten commandments comes to mind, and the concept of coveting. Some sort of unconscious self punishment for wanting it... A Guilt based fear. It comes from looking at what others have and viewing that what you have now isn't enough.
It could have been that people who had more than you always reminded you of that too.

I'm included.

Exercise

You get to have money too. You can have money too. The key is to keep letting the past go.
Decide that you're going to have money too.
That you can have money too.
Look around and see the ways that you already have money. Go into gratitude. Make a gratitude list.
When you get down, go back to your

gratitude list.
It will help you feel better, and you can ad to the list.
Be patient with your process.
It is growth, and at times it can be uncomfortable.
The gratitude list can help you stay in the comfort zone. This will help your point of attraction.

40

I'll never make money.

If you've had a lot of rejection don't give up, and this isn't designed to bum you out. Many great millionaires have been through dead end jobs, homeless, living out of their cars... then they shift and become millionaires and teach

others. Persistence is key. Don't give up.
Just keep imagining what your life will be like with it.
A core worst fear for many people is what our life will be like without it.

Persistence Pays Off.

Exercise

Keep reminding yourself that you are enough. Keep reminding yourself that you have enough.
Meditate and connect with your future millionaire self.
Ask what you have to change about yourself.
Ask what beliefs have been limiting and how to get rid of them. Get any messages that will help you.
Come back as your millionaire self.

41

I have to do something other than what I want to make money.

Millions of people are in jobs they hate. Most millionaires I've studied teach, "Do what you love and the money will come." Look at beliefs about how there aren't any good jobs. I had a friend that was bummed out about $8/ hour jobs... He said there weren't any... I told him to start looking for a $15/ hour job, and think there are lots of them... 30 days later he had a job making $16.12/ hour.

"Do what you love and the money will come."

Exercise

Think of your dream job. If you put all money aside, and could do anything,
What would you do?
What have you wanted to do since you were three?
Ask yourself what is preventing you from going for it.
This gives you clues and limiting beliefs come up.
Then you can do clearing to clear what is blocking you.
It's about fine tuning...
Making corrections to wrong thinking.
Imagine it and visualize it.
If you want to be a CEO,
Imagine yourself behind the desk.
Smell the office.

If you want to be a chef imagine yourself in a kitchen of a 5 star restaurant. Imagine owning your own restaurant.
Smell the food...see it on the plates. See the tables full.

42

I don't have enough money.

Some teach that the number one way to block your flow about money is to focus that you don't have enough. It's because you are focused on the lack of it. It's a feeling.
If you feel you don't have enough...
Step and go into gratitude. The sunset is free...enjoy it...
It doesn't matter if you're a

millionaire or not... The key is being happy.
Feel like you have enough...fake it till you make it. Surrender and the universe will guide the way.

Scratch the record.

Exercise

I learned this from the teachings Anthony Robbins.
He talks about clearing the negative beliefs or "counter intentions," as some call them. Imagine a record on a turntable.
It's playing all of the not enough songs.
Scratch the record.
Make it unplayable.
Take if off of the turntable.
The concept is you are removing it from your unconscious mind,
clearing the pattern and program.
Then put a new record on the

turntable. One that is playing the affirmations you have written or recorded for yourself.

43

Rich People are Evil.

We've been through it... get over it. Ask your higher-self to guide you. Start viewing money as your spiritual birthright. God wants you to have money. You are entitled to it, Claim and own it.
Take your power back concerning it.

Unconditional Loving.

Exercise

Look at your perception of God. Investigate your childhood.

What beliefs were handed to you.
It's just a negative stereotype.
If you had restrictive conditions as a child or punishing parents, we tend to view God that way.
We hear about, "The fear of God,"… and "Any God fearing man"... View God as this unconditional loving being that picks you up and hugs you. See yourself being apologized to for those belief systems.
It's just learning and growth. God loves you more than You can imagine.
Find the love of God and connect with it. You're loved no matter what.
The yogis talk about this is the truth that is always there. Just connect with it.
Think of God's love coming in through the top of your head.
It fills your body and permeates every cell.
Imagine that God wants you to have

money, because you are responsible and can handle it.

Imagine that you're a person that money will help make you better. You're not evil in the first place. Don't worry.

44

God wants us to struggle.

For centuries people have been creating their own suffering to get closer to God. I heard it said that if you chose to incarnate in the last 2000 years, you chose to suffer on some level.

We just shifted cycles and the next 26,000 years are a Golden Age cycle. You're not supposed to suffer. Now, you're supposed to celebrate

and rejoice.
Know you're not trapped in
perpetual suffering.
It shifts as soon as you shift focus.
Decide that you don't have to suffer
to get closer to God.

Stand in the spot light.

Exercise

See yourself standing on stage.
See how you are with all of your
beliefs about money, the part of you
that has been suffering. Imagine the
reaction of the crowd. Notice, how
you feel inside about that reaction.
Then take a bow.
That character is over.
As you do this, step out of that role.
See the audience applauding you for
playing that part. Now get excited.
Build your own money character.
Later we'll talk about dressing for
success. Fake it until you make it.

Keep becoming the person you want to be.

45

God wants us to suffer.

We adopted that belief, because we chose it. So that when we return to bliss it means more. The adage you can't know love until you've known suffering… OK, we experienced it. Thank God you made it through. Celebrate the suffering is over.

Close the book on the past.

Exercise

See the past as over now.
The old story is a book you are
going to place in your Akashic
records. Write on the book what you
want to file it under.
Imagine closing the book. Put it on
the shelf. Imagine opening a new
book.
Write on the first page how you want
it to be. You are beginning a new
story.
God wants you to succeed

46

You have to suffer to get closer to God.

It's all closely related.
It comes up again, because it had
been coded into us. Now, it's about
turning those programs off on the

unconscious level. A lot of these beliefs are similarly and closely related.

It's concepts and coding that has been in our subconscious. Now, it's sifting through whats in there.

The truth is God doesn't want you to suffer.

Buddha said that ,"Life is suffering." That's the old paradigm.

People all over the world have been celebrating the new paradigm.

The new Buddha is a laughing Buddha.

He has a plate of gold on his head, and has his hands up with a rainbow arching between them. He's happy and celebrating.

Celebrate the past is over.

Exercise

Do a celebration. Have a feast.
Celebrate the new dimension.
Do something nice for yourself.
Connect to "the spiritual grid."
Right now, people are celebrating
love and rejoicing. People are still
praying for the shift on the planet.
Many have already shifted. Connect
to the grid in meditation.
There are people there that will heal
you and send you love. There are
people that will hold the vision with
you. Celebrate suffering is over.
Imagine a chip in your brain... The
programs of suffering. Take it out.
Replace it with a new chip of the
new dimension. Heaven on Earth...
Everything you need shows up. Put
the new program in your mind.

47

Rich people don't get into Heaven.

"It's easier for a camel to get through the eye of a needle than a rich man to get into Heaven." I believe it was taken out of context. Not all rich people are bad.

He was talking about the corruption going on at the time. It's 2000 years later.

When was the airplane invited? The Wright brothers were in 1903.

Remember when the video game "Pong," came out? Now, we have fullon computers.

If you believe God loves and accepts you as an unconditional being... you get into Heaven.

Many of us want to be rich and think

that would be Heaven. It's a fine line. You hear about millionaires that aren't happy. They key is to be able to enjoy it too. Don't allow the fear that God won't accept you stop you. God wants you to have millions and be happy doing it. If you make tons of money and help a lot of people doing it, What makes you think God won't let you into Heaven?

"Say Hello to Heaven"

Exercise

Imagine getting into Heaven. You're forgiven.
Now, you have the opportunity to clear your karma. Imagine you only get this life.
You have the opportunity to be extraordinary. What are you going to do to live your dreams. You're

doing it now by reading this. Give yourself credit. You're trying. You're learning, You're growing.
The main thing is to take the panic out of it. God loves you.
What you do with life is your choice.
Imagine helping a bunch of people.
Having fun... making a bunch of money.
God thanks you.
You did it.
Thank God!

48

You have to sell your soul to have money.

Again this concept that money is a dark evil thing.
It is outside of you, and you can't have it unless you sell your soul. St.

Germain teaches, "You can't sell your soul... it's an illusion." You are you...it's how you feel inside of you. Reclaim your soul and your power to make money.

Exercise

Soul Retrieval:

Sit upright in a chair.
Place your left hand palm up.
Place the tips of fingers in your right hand together.
Place the tips of your right hand fingers in your solar plexus two inches above your belly button.

Say out loud:

I call back my soul.
All it's pieces.
Any pieces that were lost or taken away.
Any pieces that I thought I sold or gave away.
I cut the chords of any contracts or agreements I've made that aren't serving me.

(Imagine ripping up old soul contracts.) (Imagine violet fire burning them away.)

Then say:
These pieces are mine.
I claim and I own them.
I call back my soul from all timeframes and dimensions. Now, I am whole and complete again.

Imagine pieces of your soul coming back to you. Feel them seat and anchor in your chakras and your

aura.
Take a moment as they integrate.

49

Rich people are greedy.

We discussed it... that it's bad to have money and it's greedy to have a lot of it… That you having a lot and it takes away from others having a lot. The truth is that it is up to the individual and money itself doesn't care.
We create our luck. People come out of great poverty to create kingdoms of wealth for themselves. Their main message is..."You can do it too."

Volunteer

Exercise

Don't jump out of your skin.
If you think you don't have money.
You might think that you can't afford
to volunteer.

Not only is it good karma.
You meet a lot of good people.
A lot of wealthy people volunteer.
A lot of wealthy donate.
This is about changing our
perceptions of money and wealth.

Volunteer:
You'll feel better about yourself. You
can meet other wealthy people...
Make new connections.

Some talk about if you want more
give more. It's a universal law, what
you put out comes back to you.

50

Making money is a pain.

Jobs suck...poor economy...excuses. We've all had jobs we don't like. You're not stuck... keep moving find something you like better. Find your niche.

I always went for jobs at the most enjoyable places I could think of working. Make it fun.

If you're getting a job, get it at a place you would be hanging out at anyway.

Find people doing what you wish you were doing and hang out with them. There are plenty of fun ways to make money.

Make a list of all of your dream jobs.

Exercise

If you could do anything what would you do.
I've heard of people in their 80's finally singing for crowds like they always wanted to. The Key is don't wait.
Look for jobs in the field you want to be in. Find people already doing it. See if you can hang out with them. Find out what they did and model them. Challenge yourself.
If you always wanted to be a singer; and you've been hiding in your room, get out and sing in front of people.
Take the next step. It might be scary at first. You have to do it.
Find the people there that seem encouraging. You'll feel better once

you did it,
and you'll have some experience
under your belt. Next time, you
won't be as afraid.

51

Making money is hard.

The concept that you have to work
long hours at some grueling
punishing job that you can't stand.

It's true some people do get two or
even three jobs, but for many that
scares people. To a lot of people
money means not having to work.
I want to have a lot of money, so that

I don't have to work.
How can you turn your play into work?

Success experts ask the question, "What have you wanted do since you were 3?" They explain, do what you've always dreamed of.
What you wanted to do since you were 3 is what you're supposed to do.
The problem is we've been programmed we can't... do something else to have something to fall back on… then that takes all of our time, and we feel stuck there. We get mad at ourselves, because we feel like we're not doing what we're supposed to be doing.

Live Your Dreams

Exercise

Start doing what you dreamed of. Looking for jobs you like makes going to work not so bad. When you do what you love, work feels like play.
We all have a unique mission.

Mediate:
Go within.
Ask your heart. "What is my mission." Ask your heart. "What am I here to do."

Ask
"What is blocking me from acheiving my mission." "What can I do to reach my goal."

Write down any insights you get. Begin to take action steps toward your vision.

52

I have to hustle to make money.

I've tried it... I know others have to.
You can't just sit around meditate on
having a bunch of money and
expect it to show up.

Bob proctor talks about it in, "11
Forgotten Laws in the Law of
Attraction." The thing they don't
explain is you have to take action.
You have to take steps.
Success experts write down their
goals, make lists, and visualize
results.

Stay focused.

Exercise

If you want it you'll get it.
If you're unemployed look for ten jobs a day until you have one.
Many don't want to hear that.
That's hustling.
Here I'm not talking about the hustlers we see playing which nutshell is the ball under either.
I'm talking about creating your own niche and carving it.
You do have to hustle.
You have to come up with ideas and take action steps.
When you're doing it doing what you love it doesn't feel like a job.
I always decided where I was going to work and went and got a job there.
For a while, I had to turn down work, because it was coming at me from

all directions. Create it.
The perfect amount of work, the perfect job.
Find the feeling.
Hold the focus.
Your own business takes time, but you can do it.
Start now.
Instead of making it drudgery, feel good while you're doing it.
It's the fear that you will have to do all this work that sucks that stops you.
If you find fun and easy things that you like to do...
It feels more like play.

53

More money goes out than comes in.

This happened to me when injured at work.
I went from making $2000/week to $200 and some change.

Even though I was making good money, workman's comp had limits.
I was getting the max benefit.
I felt punished somehow.

You have to adapt.
I cut into my savings and eventually cashed in my annuity funds. I should have geared down and changed my life style.

I should have made pots of coffee at home rather than going out everyday for it. I didn't wan't to appear like I didn't have money...
I thought having money meant going out for coffee everyday.

Save it for special occasions. It means more.

Go check out the sunset...it's free.
Figure out ways to save money...
Cut out paying to rent movies, and
get something for free at the library.
You can still have fun if you are
creative.
Know that it is temporary.

The main thing is don't panic.
Don't cash in your annuity... you
want the feeling and knowing of
having it. That's why we're here
anyway.

Focus on being out of debt.

Exercise

The Dali Lama talks about
the quickest way to heal a problem
is to focus on the absence of the
problem. Jesus spoke about
For every sickness there is a belief
creating it.

The easiest way to explain it is.
You're not sick, you only think You're
sick.
As soon as you stop thinking it you
won't be.

Stay focused on having more money
coming in than going out. Adjust
your lifestyle temporarily.

Skip going to dinner and the bar.
Save the money,
and let your friends wonder where
you are.

Meditate on what you can do.
Try not to think.
Let your mind be silent.
Hold the focus on more money
coming in than going out.

The ideas will flash on your screen.
You'll be guided. Sometimes you
don't get it right away.

Don't get angry
That's a major key.
Stay in the having enough feeling.
Then surrender...let it go for a bit.
Sometimes you have to go do
something else to not think about it.
Then the ideas present themselves.

54

I can't handle money.

Self-discipline...
I'm working on it all the time. You
can handle! You have to.
It's about taking responsibility.
It does require being able to handle
and staying on top of it.

I'm a clean as you go type of
person.
If you always keep it clean, you

never have a mess to pick up. I used to try to explain this to my friend.

I would help him clean his house after our parties.
He would let it pile up.
I'd have to explain, if you're going to grab another beer... Just whip your empty in the recycling next to the fridge.

Why let it pile up?... just stay on top of it.

If you are already going to the fridge, save yourself some future hassles. Get in a practice of staying organized.

Organize

Exercise

Clean the closets.
Get your stuff in order.
Sell items that are collecting dust.

Yard sales, craigslist, Ebay
Donate stuff you can't sell, that you haven't used and is taking up room. This gets you clear of the past and makes room for more to come in.
Plus it is an act of keeping the flow going.
It is keep the energy circulating.
Get a system for filing papers and bills.
Balance your checkbook.
It's about making new habits.
It's an act of handling the basics and showing the universe you can handle keeping it together.
As soon as you believe you can handle money, the universe will start giving it to you.

55

I don't know what I'd do if I had money.

This is why the universe won't give it to us. You have to have a plan.

Show that you are responsible. This is why people that win the lottery and are broke in a year. They live like a king for a year then it is over.

I had to clear the fear of Cinderella, at midnight it is over fear. Be able to save and have a sense of security. If you win the lottery, take ten percent and blow it.
Get a bunch of cool stuff and step into the next level.

Buy a cool house and a cool car...then get a financial advisor and

figure out how to get bonds, ira's,
and some form of passive income.
Buy an income property and lay low.

Get a plan and put in on paper.

Exercise

Start figuring out what you are going to do.
It is sort of like a vision board.
You put down your dreams.
We've been doing this.
Keep doing it.
Start expecting results.
I think it was Andrew Carnegie who had a money formula. You think of a definite amount.
Then you come up with a plan to get it.
Then do your plan.

It is simple.
Our minds have been trained that it's hard.
It's not hard at all.
You'll see how easy it is once you actually start doing it.

56

If I have money people will be after me for my money.

I think we touched on this.

If money means a bunch of people are trying to get it from us, we can block ourselves. It's safer to just exist.
I've spent hours just being.

If you are on the planet you are contributing... You signed up and were elected to be here. We're in school spiritually.

Have fun, enjoy it.
It's the most intense time, but also the most liberating. Learn to say no. Stay in on a Saturday night and work on your business.

I helped a guy make $3000 in a day. He'd call me bummed out after going for sushi, the strip bar, and then to a hotel.

He'd be depressed and hungover. On the truth level, I'd think, "He could have stayed home."

I was working on something like this...
I used to be the guy that would buy a round at the bar and never get one in return. I'd throw the after hours party and supply everything.

Are those people going to help me with a flat tire or a jump start... Hell no! They were there, because I was the party.

If you have to buy your friends you don't want them.
It comes from wanting to look cool and get acceptance. There will be those type of people who want to glom on to you.

Others will put you down no matter what you do. Now, I read them and don't allow them in.
I don't go spend a hundred at the bar. Instead, I am typing this.
The Key is to do it anyhow. Go for your goals.

Go for your goals.

Exercise

Challenge yourself.
If you are afraid of heights do a
ropes course or tandem skydive. Do
something that challenges your fear.
It makes you stronger.
Then you're not afraid of it.
This is about becoming thick
skinned, not letting it all bother and
get to you.

Ask your higher-self to project into
your future. Plant seeds, and have
your money figure be full joy and
bliss.

Start gaining a strategy.
Plan for your future.

Protect yourself for when you are
successful.
Reframe the past.

See your past as attracting trust worthy people.

It's true, there is a lot of competition out there.

Learn to discern who is your friend and who isn't.

The idea is to be friends with everyone and have healthy relationships. That's what makes you popular.

It's not about being popular.

It's about being secure in the long run.

They tell you on the airplane to put your air mask first, before you help someone next to you. You will gain a foundation and a sense of security.

You are the one doing it.

It is up to you, and you can and will do it.

Don't let the others fool you!

57

I hate thinking about money.

To many of us money is a burden...
"You mean we have to think about
it." Especially for us artist creative
types...

 You don't have to be a starving
artist.

God doesn't want us to starve.
I've always questioned why some
artist get millions, and others get
starving. II's because of programs
and belief systems, people and
environment.
Ask yourself why... from there we
can correct it.

If money has always been a battle,
Us versus them.

They have it, and we don't.
"The System"…
If it's always been a burden...
Money this thing you can't have.
It won't accept you.
It sort of makes you sick and angry
inside.

Ask yourself, Why?

Exercise

It's true, there are a lot of old
systems that have suppressed us.
Many have tried to keep us down.
When this happens, we
unconsciously go into some sort of
self punishment. If you've ever been
abused on any level,
there is a part that believes it
deserves that abuse.

They Key is to talk to that part of
yourself. You don't deserve abuse
on any level. You deserve love and

respect.
This is what God wants for you.
When you begin to give this to
yourself, it feels like everything
rebels against you. People try to put
you in your place even more. It's
because you are shifting roles.

Tell your subconscious to stop
running all self punishment
programs.

Ask the guides and angels of the
light to assist you in DNA recoding .
They will help you.

They Key is you have to ask. That is
the rule of the Angels.

Remove:
Self-sabotage
Self-punishment
Core Level Abuse.
Self-loathing
Self-suffering

All of the negative coding of abuse on subconscious levels.

Anchor in; Self-love Self-respect, Self-confidence, Self-reassurance, and Discernment

The key is, as you feel better about yourself, help others feel better about themselves. This way they don't antagonize you in the process.

58

I hate money.

If you've had a lot of money grief, and this is a lll pissing you off... We're going to heal it.

At least you are still reading and haven't burned this book. If you are on team Robin Hood, recognize it.

If wealth is your enemy, then you won't let yourself acquire it.
You unconsciously push it away.
Remember, money is a tool.
I think of many of us, we're secretly mad at ourselves for not having it.
It's like an ex-relationship... I can't have you, so now I hate you. The truth is, you can have, at least money… first, self love.

For awile, I used to hate the word money.
Now, I'm writing a book about it.
It's because I was always programmed that I'll never have it.
Now, I teach people how to change the programs they have been running. If I can do it, so can you.

"Positive Anger."

Exercise

Thank all of the people that have
ever put you down.
Use it as motivation.
Don't fight with them.
Everything is a mirror of ourselves
teaching us something about
ourselves. Life is our teacher,
Take the anger as motivation.
When you take care of yourself,
It shows others they can take care of
themselves.
Teach through your actions.
Talk to their higher-selves.
Ask what they are teaching you.
Learn that lesson, and you can
release it.
The Dali Lama talks about asking
what it is you're supposed to learn.
They say we repeat the lesson, until
we learn it.

Ask what it is you're supposed to learn in meditation.
Then learn it, and release it.

59

Money is frustrating.

It is when you don't have it… Again, the main thing is don't panic.

Stay above the fear.
I've been homeless, now I'm writing this. Just don't go into fear.

If you are going to be a millionaire, You don't have to be homeless, as some right of passage.

The fear and lack, fight or flight, root chakra issues all deal with material and foundation. Instead of hating paying your bills do it with gratitude.

At least,you have a cell phone, and the money to pay the bill for it. Take the frustration out of it...

Taxes are taxes...
Figure out ways to be smart, and be grateful you have money to pay the bills.

Turn off the news and all of the stories of people going broke and suffering. Get in the flow with money,
Where everything always falls into place and operates smoothly.

Get in the zone.

Exercise

Take care of it, and feel good about it. Do it first, and then it is done.

When you make your to do list, take care of the easy stuff first, then you can scratch it off. Scratch it off, so you can see that you are doing something.

Green Bubble all of your money frustrations. Get it out.
Put it on paper, and then burn it.
Do this safely.
Use whatever clearing you like best.
We have to clear the frustration around money, before we'll let it in to our vibration.

60

I give up when it comes to money.

Don't give up!
This is all designed to stir up a

bunch of uncomfortable feelings then, we can clear them.
Even if you've been in a slump or downward spiral, it can be turned around over night.
Don't give up.
You will be wealthy.
On a yogi level, you already are.

Stay connected to your higher-self.

Reconnect to your higher self.

Exercise

You can do this in meditation or on the fly.
First try it in meditation, and as you get better at it, on the fly. I learned this in the 90's from the Sanaya Roman Books, Starting with the book, "Opening to Channel."

You call to your higher-self to come seat and anchor. You'll feel a click in your solar plexus.
I do this daily.

I ask my higher-self to seat and anchor…
to guide me on what to say think and do each day. From there…
You are in the state of grace.

I specialize in clearing and shifting belief systems that aren't serving any longer. Think about the things you hear.
What people are saying.
Decide if you want your unconscious mind to accept it or not.
Instead of being,
"Damned if you do, damned if you don't."
Decide,
"You're blessed if you do, blessed if you don't."

61

I'm powerless over money.

If we've experienced loss or abusive relationships... if we've had our power stripped away...

Money is only the power we give it. Historically, there has been the negative dark side of money. Now, there are people activating awakened millionaires.

We are going to turn on the wealth power and restore it in you now.

Surrender

Exercise

Clear the negative chip. Write it down and get rid of it. Do a money soul retrieval. Command your wealth power back.

This doesn't mean to get all tough and act high and mighty. This means buckle down.
Don't be afraid.
When you get quiet and ask, the angels will guide you. Follow their direction.
Every time I trust and follow the guidance of my angels, the outcome is at least 10 times better than I can imagine.

Tap your heart and say,
"I am empowered when it comes to money."
When you say it out loud it is more powerful.
If you do this in the mirror, and look in your eyes it's even more powerful.

62
When I think about money, I shut down.

It is because, we are mad at ourselves for our situation. We shut down cause the triggers are too deep… It causes too much stress. "I'll never get there...it's overwhelming." "I don't know what to do."

Make a change before you get miserable enough. Let's work on clearing the negative charge around money. Turn on the money flow, keep it open.
The trickle becomes the flow.

Open the faucet.

Exercise

Imagine the flow of money.
You can do this with your personal
energy. Visualize the amount you
have flowing. Then open and close
the valve.
Don't be afraid to ask your angels to
hurry up, but if you ask too much
you block it.
There is a period of detachment, of
letting go and trusting.

I always tell people,
"Think of all of the other times you
thought you wouldn't make it
through." "You're still here."
"Thank God."
"You're gonna get through it."
Eckhart Tolle talks about, "It's a
feeling.
If you recognize it as that,

You can allow it to pass through you quicker.

Many of us have heard, "This too shall pass."

I've heard the wave of fear generally lasts around 90 seconds.

The Key is to not resist. When you resist you fight it.
It makes you more uncomfortable.
Instead of resisting,
Do something else for a while.

John Harrircharan talks about if you're meditating and you're not getting it... It might not be the time or place.
If you change time and place the answer will come when it is supposed to. Either meditate in the same place later, or meditate some where else.

Keep the money flow open.
Ask yourself to open to receiving
and allowing.

63

The economy is poor. I can't have money.

It's true.
We've been in a depression.

Instead of being depressed,
Check out the sunset.
Then open a lemonade stand,
because they tell us, "When life
hands us lemons, make lemonade."

While the majority are talking about,
"no money and poor economy"...

There are people teaching how to thrive and make money in any economy. Listen to them.

Don't listen to the neigh-sayers.

Exercise

Find out what the current trends are, what the money makers are doing. It's not selling out to have and take care of yourself.

The Key is to not let it take you out of the present moment. One of my closest teachers taught me,
Look at your feet.
This grounds and balances you.
Realize you are all right, right now.

This will take you out of fear. The Key is to stay out of fear.

From there you can focus on why you want rather than what you don't want. This is another important Key.

The experts teach,
"Focus on what you wan't, rather than what you don't want." "We get what we focus on."

"Energy flows where attention goes."

64

Jobs are hard to come by.

Jobs are easy if you believe it. If you think,"all of the jobs are bleak," then they are.
If you believe there are plenty of good jobs then there are.

Look at the example of my friend. He was complaining about $8/hour jobs, and the lack of them. I helped him find an over $16/hr job in less than thirty days.

The first step was to look at $15/hour jobs... then see plenty of them.

There were 20 he was qualified for, and 3 he really wanted. He got the one he wanted out of 200 some applications. You'll get the job.
Don't worry.
Make it happen.

Believe you already have it.

Exercise

Write it down. Make it real. Use auto-suggestion.

We are like human computers.
First, clear the negative belief
system, then anchor in the positive
belief system.
Find the feeling.
Hold the feeling.
Release it.
Then, the ideas and action steps
come to you. Then, act on the ideas
and action steps that come to you.
Do them, and release it again.
When you're least expecting it.
It happens!

65

I can't ever get ahead.

If more is going out than coming in,
how are you? You will, as soon as
you imagine being ahead.

Stay out of fear.
Think of when it got out of balance in the first place.
If it's always been out of balance... imagine what it would have been like if it was always in balance.
Imagine being ahead.
The more you do this, then you can take the action steps without panic.
It is like heights... you're on the tight rope, and you're ok... till you look down.

Don't look down... just keep taking action steps. They have to be taken anyway, so don't freak yourself out. If you're running a marathon, you have to pace yourself. Don't panic after the first mile.

You will get ahead.
We are reconditioning ourselves to always be ahead. Look at your feet. Realize you are all right right now...

Ahead of the Game.

Exercise

Write in your notebook that you are out of debt and it feels great. This is going to be a process, so be patient. At first, don't think of how you're going to do it.
It's about, "Keeping your eye's on the prize and working backwards from there."
Put down all of the positive feelings…
"Thank God I'm out of the hole."
"It feels great to have plenty of money again."
Again, put it in terms of an exact amount when manifesting. Harlan Kilstein talks about don't just say a house, it's too general. The subconscious likes detail,

He explains, "Make it a 14 bedroom house on the beach." Stretch your imagination.
Step into it.

I did this once for a 5 million dollar house.
I wrote it down, and read it night and day.
When I was still waking up, and right before falling to sleep.
3 weeks later I was offered a place to house sit.
I got to the place, and it had everything I had written down,
A pool, spectacular views, separate yoga house, it was all better than I imagined. It just sort of happened.
It was the next day, and me and my friend were sitting outside.
He goes, "You know this is a 5,000,000.00 house."

If I can do it, so can you.
There are tons of people doing this right now, because it works.

The Key is to be specific.
I didn't write down that it was my 5,000,000.00 house. I didn't believe I could afford it.
I should have written something like, "Thank God I can easily afford a 5,000,000.00 house.

They say if you're trying to manifest a Rolls Royce, but you don't have a place to park it...
You won't allow it, and the universe won't give it to you.

You have add as much detail as possible.

EXAMPLE

"Thank God, I have a safe place to park my Rolls Royce. The insurance

is paid for a year.
I don't have to worry."

Put as much detail on the page as possible. It becomes a work book. As you do this everyday for 30 days, you keep revising it.
More idea come to you.
You see signs and signals.
Things fall into place.

They talk about this concept that happens to people when they buy a new car. You get a new car, and suddenly you start seeing other people in that same kind of car on the road. The reason is, because you are unconsciously looking to see who is driving the same car. You get what you're focused on.

66

I'm stuck when it comes to money.

If you believe you are stuck, then you are stuck.
If you believe you don't have enough, then you don't have enough.

Anything your unconscious mind believes it will accept.
We are here, because we want money... we don't know why we're not making it. It's all of these uncomfortable feelings getting in the way.
Once we clear them, we're on the fast track yo making money.
You're not stuck.

You're attracting it right now.

Take a walk

Exercise

The exercise is exercise.
Getting some circulation happening.
It might not make sense, this is a special meditation walk.

It's about opening to receive.

As you walk, keep both hands palms forward at your sides. Walking like this might challenge your security issues while you do it. It's because your energy field is open.

Before you set out for your walk, set the intent that,
"You are open to receiving." Tap your heart and say,
"I am open to receiving."

As you stroll try not to think.
Imagine just being open.

Allow whatever comes into your awareness to just be noticed.

When you breathe think of your navel. When you exhale think of the top of your head.

In Huna Philosophy this is called Pico Pico breath.

It's designed to put you in the present moment. It's kind of like two exercises combined.

The first time I tried an, "opening to receive walk," I found and Ibanez Bass amp...

Another time I found a rare 60's Gibson Tremelo tube amp.

Both were garbage picked right off the side walk. "Thank You Universe!"

I'm not guarantying what you will find... if anything.

It's about receiving and allowing... then you let the universe supply it.

It goes along with what I was explaining about surrender. "When you surrender the universe does the work."

67

I'm limited when it comes to money.

Then, you doubt all of the unlimited abundance programs being sold. I've been studying them too.

We got downloaded fear based, not enough coding from our parents who got it from their parents.

In the 20's and 30's people used to make a buck a week. Now a movie and popcorn costs $10-20.

We can complain about inflation, but even minimum wage is at more than a buck a week.

Look at the value of a dollar then compared to now.

Look at where they were coming from, and where we are coming from.

If you believe it's unlimited, then the universe surprises you.

If you vibrate lack, then you get just that.

Change your resonation.

Exercise

This is a mediation.
Sit or lay down.
Imagine a blue bubble of protection

around your aura while you are in this meditation.

Do breathing and relatxation. You can use Pico Pico breath.

Imagine going into the higher realms to a temple. It's referred to as
The Prosperity Accelerator Chamber

Here, you will meet with beings of the light that will assist you. They will take you to a room where they work on your cellar structure. It's like going into a crystal chamber. Once you're in there, they work on your resonation.
Lack and not enough are removed. The resonation of enough and more than enough are anchored. You are shown how much abundance there really is.

You will be guided.
You can ask questions and set

specific intents. When you are ready you will be guided back.

Bring the good feelings of having enough with you.

68

I'm blocked.

I just touched on that one… If you believe you're blocked then you are.

People will try to talk you out of it, and you'll get angry. It's like the whiner child, "La la la... I'm not listening."

It is because we are closing ourselves off.
Get unblocked by first believing you're not blocked.

Pick up your inner child and hug it.

Exercise

We all have an inner child.
In the first seven years of our lives is when we got downloaded most of our programs.
Anything you can shift during those years will get you better results.
It's because it's deeper foundational coding.
It's when they got installed.

Give your inner child a hug, and explain that it is safe and ok.

Fill him/her with love, and apologize for past wounds and old hurts.

Explain that you're going to be the one who mothers and fathers it.

Any time you feel that you need love, connect with your concept of Divine Mother and Father.

On a yogi level, we're getting love from the source.
This will help you and your inner child feel better inside.

That's what this is all about in the first place.

69

Money causes stress.

There is stress on both sides of money.

The stress of not having it... The stress of acquiring it.

This is why success experts talk about do what you love and the money will come. To them, work feels like play.

I could stress out on if anyone will buy or read this book. Right now, I'm enjoying sharing what I've studied and learned.

It's a matter of perspective.

Stress Free.

Exercise

Let the stress go.

Imagine all of the stress. Don't be afraid of it.

Allow yourself to feel it for a minute.

Imagine the color of it. The shape it has.

Once you have it, then be ready to let it go. Imagine a syphon in the top of your head.

It pulls the stress up and out of you.
Easily and gently.

Once the stress has been removed.
Imagine it being replaced with
golden white light.

Stress is gone.
From there the things you have to
do don't seem as if they are a
burden.

A friend of mine would make his to
do list, and everyday he would beat
himself up over not getting his list
done.

I'd try to explain,
make a realistic list and you'll feel
better.

If you don't get everything on your
list that day. You're still gonna get it.

If you stress and beat yourself up, you're not in the feeling space you need to be in.

Give yourself credit for what you are doing, rather than focusing on what you haven't done.

70

I get nervous when I think about money.

The question is where does this come from and why?

Who taught you about money? What attitude did you adopt?

What was happening in the first 6-7 years of your life?
Stop being intimidated.

As soon as you panic or get nervous you fall out of the love based feeling.

This means get in gear and do it. Just don't panic, rush, and flail through it.

As I write this book, there is the part of me that wants to hurry up an d be done with it.

I want to be selling it... I have to be honest.

Take the nervousness out of it.

Do it to do it. Do it to not stress.

Do it because you have to.
Don't think about how many you're going to sell... Think of the people you are going to help. That's what comes back to you in the long run.

Don't Panic

Exercise

Reframe the first 6-7 years of your life.

Imagine it the way you wished it would have been and how you want it to be now. Change any messages you had.

I tell people if someone beat you up and stole your lunch money. Change it.

Work it out with their higher-self.

See them apologize to you. Imagine it as if they bought you lunch instead.

Any messages that you should be uncomfortable with it or around it, change.

It's about being comfortable around money. Go hang out where people with money are.

Go sit in the expensive mall. You don't have to buy anything. Just hang out for awhile.

Observe it.
Walk through the more expensive market. Be around it.

Get comfortable with it.

71

I'm not destined to make money.

It is time to change your destiny. Where does this belief come from?

What if you were guaranteed a million dollars? What would you do? Would you be able to keep it or lose it?

Would you expand upon it, or would it disappear?

I come from a background where being a millionaire isn't possible... Don't bother and give up sort of attitudes.

This comes from the depression... Now, the baby boomers are teaching everybody should be a millionaire.

Imagine being destined for money and wealth.

You can have it. You deserve it.

You're destined for greatness... you're destined for wealth and prosperity.

Destined for Greatness

Exercise

Change your destiny. Decide you're destined for wealth.

You're already in the process, So give yourself credit.

Tap your heart:
"I am destined for prosperity, wealth, and abundance."

There is the concept that what you seek is is seeking you.

Imagine tapping into the universal flow. It's available to everyone.

If you do what the success experts say,
You're guaranteed, prosperity, wealth, and abundance.

The stronger you believe it.
The quicker you will make it happen.
The easier it will seem.

"Thank God, it's great to know," "You are now destined for wealth!"

72

It's impossible to make lots of money.

...Limiting! It's totally possible!

The key that millionaires all talk about is that they expect it.

Expect it...feel it...be it... View yourself as a money miracle.

You are it externalizing it.
This is what the sun and moon mediation is about.

Just identify yourself with the thing you want to manifest. Surprise yourself with your own money miracle.

Become it.

Exercise

In the movie "Caddy Shack" Chevy Chase talks about, "Become the Ball."
It's true.
Tiger Woods visualizes where the ball is going to land before every shot.

This is a visualization, become the money you want to manifest.

We sort of touched on this earlier. This is where you identify with it.

To take it a little deeper,
it is sort of scary the first time.

You let go of the concept of you as a person momentarily.
You step into becoming the amount of money or thing you want to manifest. These techniques can be used to manifest more than just money, and money is more than just paper.

Look at all of the internet transactions, it's money in space. Just numbers bouncing around... it's not tangible.

Feel what it is like to be a million dollars.
I've done this more than once, and manifest $1000-$1500 in 24 hours.

From this place and concept, there is no difference between a buck and a million bucks. They're in the ethers.

The yogis talk about bringing it from one plane of existence to another.

The place of existence, where everything is.

Try it.
Identify with a buck. Identify with a million bucks.

They feel different.
The more you can hold the feeling of the thing it is you want. The quicker you can manifest it, because you are in energetic alignment.

If you are the million bucks... You already have it.

The Key is trying it first with things that you think are easy to start.
That's why I tried $1000 at first.
When I did it again,
It jumped to $1500.
(The intent was, at least $1000)

Try it with a buck.
Identify with a dollar for as long as you can.

What does it think? What does it feel? Then be it. You are it. You have it now.

Then release it. Forget about it.

Don't be surprised when you manifest one real easy. It just happens...
the universe supplies it in its own way.

Don't lose the feeling of having it. You still have it...
Until you have it.

The Key is holding the feeling that you think that thing will bring you. If you can do that, on one level you don't need it.
On another level, you have it already.
Then you're in energetic alignment with it, and the universe makes it happen.

Like attracts like. You attract it to you.

73

Only a select few get to have money.

The Elitism belief system.
"The rich get rich, and the poor stay poorer."

Shift the belief that you are poor.
Focus on the ways you are wealthy already.

It's unconscious...
this is about clearing what has already been drilled into the mind, and anchoring something new.

Tony Robins talks about clearing the old program first.
You can't play a record on a

turntable if there is already a record on it... I think I already spoke about scratch the records.

Here's another one for the difficult ones.

Use a jack hammer!

Exercise

This is figuratively.

Do a meditation and imagine the belief system that you are poor.
We hear of "Breaking blocks all day." This book is all about breaking the subconscious blocks that are holding you back.

Imagine a pile of cinder blocks.
"They say: "You're poor."
"You were born that way." "You have no luck." "Negative money beliefs."
"Not enough money to go around."

Take the jack hammer to it. Imagine breaking the beliefs and memories.

It's fun and easy. You feel good doing it.

Break any walls if you have them.

Once you have a big pile of sand. Imagine building a sand box. Fill it with the things you want.

Tell your subconscious mind to bring you more of these good feelings.

74

It's shameful being rich.

Why?
The negative connotation...

Guilty... for what?

"Guilty pleasure"... "Filthy Rich"...
Negative programming.

We created that as a setback
somewhere in evolution.
The systems where the king had all
of the money and we were all
peasants.

Now, it's fair game. Everyone is
entitled. Tap in.

When you work towards it and earn
it, then you feel worthy and
deserving.

Don't let guilt prevent you.

Think of helping the people with it.
If you're happy, it teaches others
they can be happy too.

Having is not bad. Don't let your
sensitive chords get played.

Raise your hand.

Exercise

I was at a Mega Wealth Convention and Robert Allen and Mark Victor Hanson say, "Who wants a hundred dollars?"

Out of a couple of thousand people, about a hundred raised their hands.

They gave it to the first person who raised their hand. At the time, I didn't raise my hand, and I wished I would of. I was afraid.

Raise your hand.
Declare you are open to receiving money, wealth, and abundance.

If you say,
"I wan't money,"
it's still focus on the lack of it.

While your hand is up,
Thank the universe for all you have ever had.
Ask to be guided on the steps to take to get to where you want to be.

Put your hand down and imagine your brain being washed with clean rainbow light. Imagine all of the shame, guilt,
and negative associations with money dissolving.

You're getting a bright new money attitude.
Ask your subconscious mind to start seeing things from a fresh perspective.

75

If I have money, I'll lose my friends.

I've gone through this. Because, when you go get money, some of your friends feel abandoned. "Misery loves company"... We've all heard it.

It is called the crab bucket theory, and it's proven.

If a crab tries to crawl out of the bucket, all of the other crabs try to cling to it.

They don't want it to be free,
It registers to them abandonment.

Don't tell your drinking buddy you're going to quit drinking.

He'll cling to you and try to prevent you... who wants to lose a friend?

Find people already successful to be your friends.

They'll lift you up and won't be angry at you for achieving.

Cut out what isn't working, and bring in what does.

Detach with love.

Exercise

You sort of slip away from some, and connect to those that you know are supporting you.

When you get that brand new dream job, You start meeting new people.

Some of your friends get jealous.

You went from hanging out with nothing going on to suddenly having it going on again.

Cut the chords.

Imagine that there are chords attaching you to people place or things. Like energetic strings.

Imagine a blue sword of fire cutting those strings. Fill in where they were with golden light.

This will help you feel free'r You are changing your resonation.

You're going from hanging out with people that don't have money to hanging out with people that do have money.

The idea is to be able to hang out with all walks of life, but that doesn't mean you have to walk with all walks of life.

In the end, your true friends will still be your friends.

76

If I have money others won't.

You having money doesn't take away from others having money. It's a matter of perception.

The unlimited storehouses of abundance are available for us all to tap into. Many people limit their flow, because they don't want others

to go without. The truth is you not having doesn't help you or them.
If there is enough for all, there is no reason to go without.
If you perceive everyone can have enough, this takes the guilt out of it.

Meet your Guides and Angels.

Exercise

For me, I've definitely used Guides and Angels.

Do a meditation, and ask to meet them. Get their names if you can. Ask them what they want you to know.

Many of us have rogue guides and impostors.
Ask St. Germain and Archangel Michael to clear your energy field.

They have what's called an 18 point clearing.

They go through more than your main 7 chakras. They clear you in hands, feet, elbows, and hips, 18 points of your chakra system.

Call in a new team of guides, pick special ones and ask them to work with you. They love to serve and will help you.

They are always there, but there is one rule. You have to ask.

Here are some you can work with…
Archangel Chammuel, St.Germain, Abundantia, Lakshmi, The Maha Chohan, Midas

Always thank your Guides and Angels, it shows them respect.

77

I'm afraid I'll never have money.

Sigh a sigh of relief that you are correcting the patterning, making new positive money choices, and becoming financially free!

Stop being afraid, start welcoming, and start accepting.

You have money now. You already have money...

You will have the money... if you do something to stop chasing.

That's why you're reading this.

Draw the line.

Exercise

Take out a piece of paper.
Draw a line down the middle.
At the top left write "Money Fears"
At the top right, "Good Money"
"Everyone wants to make good money."

In the left column write all of the fears that come up.

In the right column write all of the new positive money beliefs.

When you are done, cut the page down the middle.

Say a prayer and ask your subconscious mind to let the money fears go.

Keep the Good Money,
Positive Money Beliefs side of the
paper.

Place it somewhere you can see it...
on your money shrine.
On the counter where you can see
it. You can carry it and read it, or put
it In a prayer bowl.

It keeps reminding your
subconscious mind that this is what
you want it to work on for you.

78

Money slips through my hands.

This stems from a past money
trauma.

A time you lost it, or someone took advantage of you.... An unexpected bill.

When I've gotten in the zone, I've had the opposite... unexpected money shows up.

Forgive yourself for past money mistakes.

Ask your future money master higher self to guide you.

Exercise

If you imagine money like water, it's supposed to flow.
You still want your water tank, but allowing it to flow is part of it.
We've all made money mistakes, don't let the past fear stop you.
Many successful people fail over and over until they get it. Try several things,

Try having what they call multiple streams.
The idea is to get money flowing in from a few different sources.

Meditation:
Money faucet.
Imagine the money valve from above. When you are feeling not enough, open the money faucet up.

79

Money is a curse.

This comes from the fear that it causes problems... turns you evil.

Middle ages.

It's a blessing if you're grateful for it.
It's a matter of belief and perception.
View money as working for you...

Acquire enough to get it working for you...

Then you have freedom.

I'm supporting you... there are no money curses.

Money is a blessing!

Exercise

Clear the belief in curses.
There are layers of consciousness.
In some layers the curses seem totally real.
In other layers, they're not real and can't touch you. Here's where the term,
"Rise above it," comes from.
Try Yoga and Tai Chi other energy practices. Maybe, this is why they say exercise your demons. Get exercise
Think about it,

If you're out jogging,
You really don't feel like anything is
going to hurt you. Hop on a bike
take a ride,
especially when you're pent up
about money. Clear your mind.
Let it go for a minute.
Then the next step comes to you.

80

I'm going broke.

They tell us to go for broke, but don't
consciously accept that.

Going broke is not the goal.

If you're broke, don't hate yourself.

Plenty of millionaires have been
broke.

"It's just a feeling. It will pass."

This is about catching and stopping the cycle. Turn, I'm going broke into I'm getting rich.

Find the people that will support this, and avoid the people that want to block you.

No one wants to block you, and the universe wants you to be rich. Go for broke...just don't let it happen.

If it did happen, you can shift overnight. It's already in you, you have money.

"Trash into Treasures."

Exercise

Turn your hobbies in to cash It's an ebb and flow.

If you go into panic, you plummet. We're going to prevent that.

Many millionaires have done it. They've lived on rice and ramen. At one time we had four guys living in a studio to save money.

This doesn't mean go live in a tent. I know plenty of anti-establishers are doing that. I agree, there is nothing like the stars, but what happens when it rains? Setting up a camp is constant work.

If you're gonna work, work smarter.

Let out the sails, and slow down.

First, stop focusing that you're going broke. Stay in gratitude for what you have. Don't view it as a bad thing. Then turn it around.

Keep holding the focus on when you had the most money. Hold that feeling.
Don't allow yourself to go into, "Not enough."

If you're sailing, the winds may change, but that doesn't mean the ship is sinking.

Think of creative ways to keep money coming in. Start an online business.
Investigate affiliate marketing.
Check out drop shipping.

———

Sell on Ebay. Do craft fairs.
Give music lessons.
Sell your paintings.
Give golf lessons.

Caddy just for exercise.
Tune bicycles.
I have a friend that details cars at a
dealership. during the day,
and then out of the garage at his
house, at night for his own clients.

Have fun.
Most of the time this is what you
want to be doing anyhow.

Love and forgive yourself. Stop
thinking you're going broke.

Stay in gratitude for what it is you
want to manifest.

81
I'm broke and stuck.

Millions of people are...
the truth is you're not broke or stuck.

It's an attitude of expectance.... A
knowing that you'll be ok.

The main thing is don't fight it.
You start thinking that you're broke
and stuck, then you get angry and
pissed... at least I do.

Anyhow, the key is to not go down
that path. Change the radio station
in your mind.

Put the puzzle together.

Exercise

Imagine putting the puzzle back together. Each piece fits together nicely.

It's symbolic of putting your life back together. You could even get an actual puzzle.

When you work on it, it will put you in the present moment. Set the intent that the ideas and action steps come to you. Keep your notebook close to write any ideas that come to you.

Imagine that each piece you put together brings you closer to wealth. It also magnetizes and attracts wealth to you.

In meditation you can visualize a puzzle all put together. This reminds you that it is all worked out.

You're working and having fun at the same time. Put the puzzle pieces of your life together.

82

I'm not good enough to have money.

On a yogi level, you already are everything.

The belief that you're not good enough means you are not connected to your higher-self.

The truth is God loves you more than you can imagine. God wants you to have your hearts desires.

The fear that we won't get it overrides us, so we never start.

Reconnect to your higher-self. I think that's what go for broke means.

When you're already broke, you have nothing to lose. Maybe it's the fear of having it or what it takes to get it.

If you follow your heart and live your dreams you will achieve them.

Go for broke, but clear that from the unconscious mind too.

See your self as worthy and deserving.

You are the million that you want. Once you identify with it, then you can manifest it.

Reconnect

Exercise

Ground your energy from your tailbone to the core of earth. Setting the intent will do this.

Imagine a ball of white light 12 inches above your head. This is the chakra that your higher-self comes in through.

Imagine reconnecting as if there is a spiral of light that comes down from that ball of light through your spinal column.

Imagine your higher-self seating and anchoring. It connects in your solar plexus,
and spreads down into your legs into your feet. It spreads into your arms and hands, and it fills your entire body.

Connect with the part of you that is good enough.
Have it work in your solar plexus to increase self-confidence and self-esteem.

83

I'm not willing to do what it takes to make money.

It's because we believe in this bleak existence.

I can work two lame ass jobs... it won't get me there.

Success experts teach that's not the way. That will get you through in the meantime…

Many musicians have heard, "Don't quit your day job."

You have to have income, true. Use how much you can't stand it as motivation towards your goal. Napoleon Hill talks about positive anger in "Think and Grow Rich." This is about becoming un-brainwashed.

Then use the motivation to do it. Change your perception.

I was in a shaman class, and we looked at the spirit of money. The energy was feminine like a tall beautiful woman.
It likes play, and it moves quick.

I think of when I used to bartend, money is constantly flowing... the till keeps bing bing binging.
It's not a depressed energy.

In other classes we did money dances.

I went from homeless to having a place to live and $1500 once, by going out alone in nature and jumping around like I was at a rock concert and going,

"Thank God I have a place to live and money in the bank." Make it fun... you have to be into it.
It's making it so real that you trick your brain, and then it happens.

Shake it off.

Exercise

Get out of wrong thinking and low energy. Jump around shake off the stress. Some shamans do this to get ready for healing ceremonies.

It's about lifting your vibration.

Start affirming:

"I have what it takes to make money." "I will do what it takes to make money."

Classes like ecstatic dance are a great way to get the experience of this. You just let your body move how ever it feels like moving.

Do your celebration dance of having money, before you have it. This is putting you in the energetic feeling of having it.

Do a money dance.

Meditate and talk to your version of the spirit of money. For you it could be something completely different. What is it like? What does it want to teach you? What do you need to know?
What do you need to shift and

change about yourself? You have to
be willing to shift and grow.

84

You have to work hard scramble, suffer, and pursue money.

I believe this goes back to cave
man... primal fear.
It sucked,
some days you might not get
anything days... feast or famine....
fight or flight... root chakra.

It's about getting some money and
making it work for you. Financial
planning.

If you're still stuck on all the jobs suck and millionaires are a different breed, we have to clear it.

It's conditioning. We're shifting the program.

Money Magnet

Exercise

Magnetize yourself for money. Imagine it coming to you, rather than chasing after it. think in terms of, "It's rainy money!"

There is plenty it flows easily.

Florence Shovel Shin had an affirmation. "I am an irresistible magnet for money."

Remember the times when you had good harvests.
For me it was picking wild raspberries with my friends and

brothers as a kid. It's about finding the good feeling,
remembering the good memories.

Think of the past money miracles.
I just had a friend that was in money panic. She was down to $17.
I told her not to worry, stay out of panic, you'll work it out.
You will get through.

The next day she called me.
She had found $170 that she hid and forgot she had.

One time I was bar tending, I was worried I couldn't pay rent and bills.
I went to work hoping and praying for a good night. That night a homeless looking dude gave me $100 tip. It was the extra few bucks to cover what I needed.

It's a matter of perception.
$100 seems like nothing to some

people To me, at the time, it was a matter of life or death.
At, least it felt that way.

When you can't figure it out on your own surrender. Ask your guides and angels to help you.
A big key is getting quiet and trusting.

You will be guided.

85

I don't deserve money.

Since when and why?... Those are the questions to ask yourself.

Once we uncover that, then healing of the past will help.

See it the way you wished it would have been and the way you want it to be now. You deserve money... accept it.

Cellular Restructure

Exercise

Write in every cell of your body.

"I deserve money."
Imagine your cells with smiley happy faces. Put your own affirmations in as well.

It's changing the cellular structure to go from not deserving to deserving. Use green light to heal your cells and clear negative messages and memories. As the green light absorbs the negativity, it becomes murky with the old emotions.

Open the portals in your feet chakras, and have the negativity

pour out.
As this happens imagine a fan overhead.
It sucks the negativity up and out of the room to be transmuted.

Then, imagine your cells filling with rainbow golden light. It nourishes your cells and fills you with good feelings. Have it anchor in self-worth and deservingness.

86

I don't know how to make money.

That's because no one ever taught us.

It's ok, forgive them. Congratulate yourself, because you learning now.

Surround yourself with wealthy people, read success books,
Give yourself credit for doing what you're doing... you're here.

There is a part of you that knows how to make money.
They talk about connect with your future millionaire and work backwards.

Educate your self.

Exercise

Books, trade manuals, school, continued education, and personal mentors.

Every success expert I have studied has talked about the use of a mentor. They've done it.
They have experience.
They can point out what you're not seeing for yourself.

Successful people have support around them. Other like minded people.

The more you learn the more you grow, then you can help others.

For everything you are struggling with there is a book to teach you how to overcome it.

Don't be intimidated.
It's a process.
You are learning how to make money.

87 Money is a sin.

Hopefully, you still don't believe this one.

For many of us, it is deep in our unconscious. We hear about sinful delights again, guilty pleasure.

There are plenty of spiritual millionaires that got over this one. You can become one too.

Kneel and pray.

Exercise

This is act of reverence and respect. It is observed in many religions. Apologize for taking on these belief systems. Ask for forgiveness. Ask to be corrected. Ask to be washed clean.

Imagine being re-baptized. Imagine being forgiven. Start new. View money as a blessing and a miracle. Money is your birthright.

88

Being rich is a sin.

I don't know where this comes from at this point. Still based in the fear of money being evil, that the rich are bad.
I'm gonna call it Robin Hood Syndrome." Even the pun in the name Robbing Hood, as if the wealthy are all hoods...

It's not a sin, so begin.
We're taught not to get our hopes up... this is about keeping our hopes up. It's a resonation.

Erase the blackboard.

Exercise

"Erase it from your mind."

This is a common technique used by psychologist, hypnotist, and healers. You imagine the thought or belief on a black board.
Once you do that erase it.

After you have erased the self-limiting belief from the black board, write a new positive belief on it 50 times.

This helps anchor the new belief.

89 Money is dirty.

Again... Filthy Rich! "Eat the Rich"

It stems from a resentment of wealth. They have it w e don't.

They obviously did something bad to get there. It's separation.
Underneath the anger is sadness. We're mad a wealth, because we don't have it. Inside, we're deeply feeling sadness and unworthiness. When you stop making it the enemy, money welcomes you. Wash clean of negative beliefs around money.

"Rinse and Repeat."

Exercise

Imagine your energy field is like a percolator.

Turn on a cleansing program that clears this.
The old beliefs bubble up and out of you and float away.

You're being revitalized and recharged. imagine your soul being nourished and replenished, You're getting what you need energetically.

Have a hose with golden white light rinse this out of your system. It's anchoring clear new money ideas, beliefs, and direction.

90 I'm poor.

It's conditioning for many.
Be the one that steps out and steps up.

Stop thinking poor.
Fake it till you make it.
It sounds hokey, but they've all done it.

Some teach dress for success.
Instead of never wearing your favorite shirt, Start wearing your

favorite shirt.
You'll feel better.

Notice how other people are.
Practice being comfortable around
money.

Meditate and go to the Karmic Board.

Exercise

There is a temple in the higher
dimensions.
You ask permission to go in. There
you will enter and meet with the
Karmic Board.

Ask them to rescind any past life
poverty vows and any other vows
that aren't serving you. Then, there
is a place there to light a candle.
Trust your prayers are being
answered.

91

Poor people are more happy.

I learned how to be happy being poor, but it still sucks.

Isn't it better feeling as if you can go to a movie without wondering if you should? It's true, you can check out the sunset and be happy.

We got used to being poor.
We got convinced, there's no choice.

If you believe it's all hassles and stress, you'll block it.

Imagine taking your family on vacation or buying a new home. Smell the new paint as you walk in.

This is about being happy in the process and to have more to enjoy life with. Imagine being able to have something to pass on to someone.

"Don't Worry Be Happy."

Exercise

If you've already learned to be happy being poor, then you have half of the battle over.

It's all about being happy.

The song "Don't Worry Be Happy," by Bobby McFerrin popped into mind. It puts you in a feel good space, and it's a positive affirmation. Play your own happy songs, but still get stuff done.

Rock out while you clean the house.
Listen to positive money affirmations
while you're paying the bills.

Work is work, but you can still have
fun in the process.

Look at many of the mega wealthy.
Many are doing what they love, and
they have a blast.

Step out of the brain washing.
Use the technique of imagine your
brain being washed clean.

One of my old bosses always used
to say, "Getting there is half the
battle."
He was referring to work.
You don't want to go,
but once you're there it's not that
bad. We actually had a lot of fun at
work.

Get up and go.
If you do it you'll feel better.

When the paycheck comes it is worth it. That's why Nike's slogan is, "Just do it."

I explain to my clients, it's like standing on a dock waiting to dive in a lake. There is that moment when you are nervous and think the water is going to be cold. You have to take the plunge and get that moment of discomfort,
before you get used to the water. Once you do, it's refreshing.

This is the same thing. It's temporary.

Even though it scares you do it anyway.
They say all of the ideas are out there for everyone to tap into. Many people get the thought, but few act on it.

The ones who act on it are the successful ones. Why? Because they did it.

92

There's a shortage of supply.

If you're into eastern philosophy, you can talk and work with Lakshmi the Goddess of Abundance.

Ask her to work with you... start seeing abundance.

It's the cup half full sort of thinking. It's unlimited. Keep reminding yourself.
You can also work with the Maha Chohan and the Universal Storehouses of Abundance.

Ask the universe for supply.

Exercise

Notice abundance.
Some teachers talk about focus on things like the abundance of air.
How water comes out of a faucet.
The abundance of blades of grass in your yard.
The abundance of gravel on that path.
When you start seeing and recognizing abundance, this takes you out of thinking in terms of lack.
It's a way of staying calibrated to. "there is enough."

There is also an amount of emotional detachment with this.
Your life and happiness aren't dependent on if you're a millionaire

or not. You can stay in the state of grace and be happy.

Now that you're in an abundant feel good place, then you can do your affirmations and act as if.
It's a perfect space for using gratitude for what it is you want to call in.

93

If you work hard, you'll never be rich anyway.

It's because of wrong thinking, wrong environment, not knowing how to go about it.

You can do it, but you have believe in yourself.

It takes time and energy. The exchange of goods or services.

When you work a job, you're exchanging services.

If you don't believe you're ever going to be rich, you won't try.

What if it was your destiny?

Put on your headphones.

Exercise

I had the,
"La la la, "I'm not listening visualization."
Don't listen to the neigh sayers.
If you listen to them, you'll never try.
The truth is, if you follow them you won't get there.
Follow the experts already doing it.
Sometimes, I'm changing what

people are saying to me in my head, on the fly, while they are saying it to me.

This is the act of changing the tracks.

Make your own affirmations out of all of the work you have been doing.

You can record them on your cellphone.

You can record them on your laptop or i-pad.

You can get a simple voice recorder for $20-$30.

The Key is: Guess What?

Doing it.

94

Jobs suck.

I know it came up, but look at how much negative drilling we've had around money.

Instead of looking for an $8 an hour job look for a $30 an hour job. Think in terms of going for the manager position right away.
Some people talk about if the job is $10/hr try to get $12 before you start.

Convince them you're going to a great job and that you're worth it. Jobs don't suck, finding good ones sometimes does... only if you believe that. Again, my friend was looking at $8/hr jobs... I helped him find a $16/hr job.

The key was to look and start seeing them.

Think Big

Exercise

Find a better job

Don't wait to you get fired or end up quitting. Don't wait until you're out of work. Most people just do their job, and then they want their free time.

They're not thinking that they can do something else or find something better. I can't imagine working my whole life at a job I hated. I respect the ones who do, because it's a major level of commitment.

With upper end jobs, it's worth it. You get insurance and annuity funds.

If you're not getting that already, Look for a job that will give you that.

If you get clear, decide what kind of job it is, and how much you make doing it, you'll get it a lot quicker.

Then it's not like looking through the paper at all of the jobs you don't want to do. That just ads to your stress.
When you decide,
"I'm gonna go get a job over there."
You feel more in charge of your life.

If they don't have a job right away it doesn't mean you won't get one. It's about building relationships.
If you keep checking in, and showing you're eager to work, you'll get the job.

I've had employers give me jobs when they weren't hiring, because I kept showing up asking to work.
They finally created a job, and welcomed me aboard.

The Key is not to be a pest and show up too often. Do not to let it slip by and let them forget about you either.

95

Money is a pain in the neck.

Go back to gratitude while paying the bills. Stay on top of it.

Get a system.
Instead of throwing all of your receipts in a shoe box and dealing with it late. Do it every month.

Make it fun that you're organized and on top of it.
If money is a pain, you'll avoid it.
Imagine paying your bills then going to get yourself a massage.

"Whistle while you work."

Exercise

We've talked about finding ways to make it fun.
Think of how to work smarter.
I like to listen to affirmations while I'm working on the stuff I don't like.
This way, rather than focusing that it sucks, and i don't want to do it,
I'm doing it, and thinking of something positive.
Hypnotists talk about when you're watching TV, driving in a car, or doing things like paper work,
we're already in a state of hypnosis.
Have you ever driven anywhere, and then didn't really remember the ride?
It's because you're in the present moment thinking about driving.
Many success experts listen to their

affirmations on their way to and from work.

Some affirmations say you can listen to while driving. Other ones put you into relaxation and will tell you not to listen to while driving.
The point is, on a certain level, you've been hypnotized to think money is a pain in the neck.
This is about shifting that unconscious coding to believe it's fun and easy, so you can whistle while you work.
Then you can afford that massage, and it's not such a pain in the neck after all.

96
You have to break your back.

Louise Hay talks about lower back problems being related to fear of money. That's an old term.

"Working on the chain gang," belief systems come to mind as well. I hurt my lower back on a job once.

When I think about it, on some level, I didn't want to do that job.

Don't get hurt at work, and think you're gonna get a bunch of money.

From my experience:
Workers Compensation tries to hassle and screw you... You might get less than you were making, and you go back to work injured. At least, I did.

It is because they didn't want to pay to heal me in the first place, so I didn't end up getting what I thought you should. You're could end up worse off than you were. I didn't get hurt on purpose, but I believe there was a subconscious reason for it.

It's about finding your niche, a unique product or service that fires you up. I had jobs I hated going to, and jobs I didn't want to leave.
You can make good money in things like construction, just stay safe.

While you're doing it, figure out how to become the contractor.

Save your health.

Exercise

Many wealth experts talk about the number one thing that makes you wealthy is your health.
"If you're not healthy, then you can't enjoy it anyway."

I think they go hand it hand.

When you're energetically strong, you feel better.
If we are explaining that the way to attract wealth is by staying in a feel good space, then health is a big Key.

I've been challenged financially and physically. When I look at the themes in my life, when I have been challenged financially, I was going through physical challenges as well.

If you are going through this, call on your own power to overcome.

See that there is light at the end of the tunnel.

I tell people to visualize themselves coming out of the tunnel into the light. Visualize the tunnel close behind you.
You have stepped out of your, "darkness before the dawn."

Drink some water, get some exercise, do something good for yourself. You deserve it!

97

I don't have any money.

When you get excited and don't give up... you're rich. I've heard, "Heaven on Earth is no thoughts"... don't think about it.

Keep thinking of having money,
I like to imagine the smell of it.
You are in the process of becoming
a money master...imagine that.

10 minutes a day.

Exercise

An exercise I learned from Nelson
Barry at Subliminal Wealth is to
focus on it for 10 minutes.
As you start your day give yourself
ten minutes.
You clear your mind and spend 10
minutes thinking of what you can do
to make more money.
Just relax about it.
Take some deep breaths.
You can do this while you have your
coffee.
Write down all of the ideas that
come to you.
Begin to take action steps on what
comes to you.

Stay in the good feeling of having, while you're doing it.

98

It is tough times.

You heard it. "When the going gets tough, the tough get going."
Those are the people who thrive in any economy. If others can do it so can you.

"Don't let the times fool you"... Don't listen to the negativity around you. The times are shifting, anyhow.

It shifts for the better or the worse... depending on what you are creating.

Again, remember to focus on what you want rather than what you don't want.

Step into the new dimension.

Exercise

This goes beyond everything that you have always heard. You have to believe in miracles to receive miracles. science is beginning to figure out how and why miracles work.

If you believe times are tough, and we're in the one of the worst depressions it's true. Instead of dwelling on it,
think of it as a shifting of the times. Get excited about entering a new golden age cycle. Start looking for how things in the world are improving. Turn the news off.

When people are down and depressed, I tell them to watch a lot of comedies.
The Marx Brothers movies have been known to cure cancer.

Get excited and motivated. Start living your passion. Carve your niche. Stop waiting.

When you're in a state of gratitude and awe, When you're focused on how great everything already is, you're not worried about the times at hand.

We see what we want to see.

If you have a project you're working on that you don't want to do, you feel like you're forcing yourself to try to do it.
You're not in the right mind frame. You can't find the tool you need. Nothing is working right.

It's because you really don't want to do it in the first place.

On the day you decide, it has to be done. I'm going to do it.
I have to do it. I'll feel better once I get this out of the way.
You look for the tool you need, and it's in a spot you've checked everyday for three weeks.
The reason is, is now, you're ready to use the tool and do the project.
You're in the right mind frame.

Notice your own mind-frames and moods.

When you're hitting the wall of resistance and it's not working... do something else for awhile.
step away and come back to it.

It's about being in the flow or not being in the flow.

When you're in the flow, you go to the mall and you get the front row parking spot.

When you're not in the flow, you go to the mall and someone takes your parking space.

Always sort of tune in with yourself, and gauge whether you're in the flow or not.

The Key is to stay in the flow, "Then time is of the essence."

In quantum physics, there is no time. This is why they explain hold the feeling of having it all ready. Many Yogis are quantum physicist whether they realize it or not. Some call it the laws of the universe.

Don't worry about what time it is. It is not real anyhow.

Step beyond it.
There are ways to speed up and slow down time through your perception. This is the next dimension.

99

I really don't want to have money.

I think we get convinced we can't have it, so we don't want it.

We do want it, but we are convinced we can't have it.

Don't get discouraged.

There is a part of you that wants it, because you're reading this book.

Remember, these are unconscious beliefs that could be limiting you. Whatever the strongest belief that is in the subconscious wins.
That's why this is designed to clear the conflicting beliefs or counter intentions.

It's about coming into energetic alignment with it, but also clearing the subconscious filters preventing it.

On some level,
Your subconscious is always doing what is necessary to protect you and keep you safe.

Ask yourself why don't I want to have money?

Star of David

Exercise

Merge your higher and lower self.

This is about overcoming duality. We all have a light and dark side.

Universal Cosmic Law is that there only two things: Fear or Love

It's about coming into balance with different aspects of yourself.

In Meditation:
Think of your lower chakras as a pyramid facing up. Think of your upper chakras as a pyramid facing down.

Now, merge the two pyramids and interlace them, so they become like the Star of David with your solar plexus as the center point.

The bottom chakras represent your conscious-self (lower self.) The upper chakras represent your higher-self.
You have merged your higher and lower self.

Ask your higher-self to work with your lower self to clear the limiting beliefs blocking you. The subconscious is the filter that goes between the two.
Ask to have your subconscious cleared of belief systems blocking you.
Have your higher-self heal your lower self, and ask your Guides and Angels to assist you in this process.

100
Money will make me worse.

Only if you let it… if you let your ego get control of you.

It happens to a lot of people, and then they lose it.

I did that once.
Let me save you the hassles.
Stay humble, stay smart, be a little conservative.

Money will make you a better person, and afford you the luxury of a better lifestyle. Turn off the unconscious fear that it will make you worse.

Money Wheel.

Exercise

On a piece of paper draw a circle. In the middle of the circle, write all the ways you believe money will make you a better person.
Outside of the circle write all of the

ways, you think money will make you worse.

Notice which has more when you are done.
If you have more reasons you think it will make you worse,
the challenge is to come up with more reasons it will make you better.

The goal is to have the center outweigh the outside.

Once you have come up with more reasons why you believe it will make you better, then you can cut the circle out.

Say a releasing prayer, then throw away the old reasons why you think it will make you worse. Keep the circle with the list of reasons money will make you a better person. Place it where you can read it.
It will help remind you money isn't bad at all.

101

No matter what I do I won't make any money.

I've been caught in that slump a few times. It's a matter of thinking.

Catch yourself.. wake yourself up out of it.

I've done it like literally switching a switch in my head.

You're not in a slump. You will make money.

You already have money, you are the money you seek, God wants you to have it.

It's your birthright.

Through your thoughts and feelings
you can begin to attract it rather than
chase after it.
Ask Midas to work with you.

Become a person that everything
you do makes you money, so that
you have enough money that you
don't have to worry.

Pot of Gold

Exercise

Imagine that you're the pot of Gold
at the end of the rainbow… that you
have shifted… that your life changed
for the better… that you did it!… that
the thing you've been chasing has
always been in you all along… that
you don't have to worry at all.
Everything has been taken care of,
and it's all worked out.

Feel what it's like to be totally content, to not have to think about it.

_____

Feel that feeling of joy. Feel the feeling of bliss.

Imagine every time it didn't work out as if it did work out. Imagine that you don't even have to worry about it, because it's all worked out.
Give yourself a pat on the back.
You made it through.
Tap your body, and anchor this feeling.
Thank God.
"You did it!"

Thanks for being here and for your unique contribution to the planet.
You are worthy, valuable, and deserving.
You have already started to make a difference.
Heaven on Earth is right now.

With a warm welcome, you've been accepted!

Made in United States
Orlando, FL
29 June 2023

34633423R00141